The Good Life in Galicia 2018

An Anthology of Prose and Poetry

www.cyberworldpublishing.com

This book is copyright © S Bush 2019
First published by Cyberworld Publishing in 2019
Cover design: Copyright Cyberworld Publishing 2019
Cover photo: Copyright: S Bush 2016

E-book ISBN: 978-0-9953961-7-3
Print ISBN: 978-0-9953961-8-0
All rights reserved

The Good Life in Galicia 2018

An anthology of Prose and Poetry

Edited by S Bush

Published by
Cyberworld Publishing

Contents

GALICIA–LAND OF FAMILY AND HISTORY

AN INTRIGUING LIFE IN GALICIA

ABOUT THE AUTHORS

Cover Image

This year's cover image is of a bodega in an abandoned village on the banks of the river Minho in the Ribeira Sacra (Sacred Riverbank) region of Galicia. It also sits directly on the official Galician hiking trail along the river, PRG 162. There are innumerable such stone buildings in various states of repair and disrepair in the area, often looking romantically attractive, as this one does, with its artistic decoration of vegetation.

Abandoned bodega behind Casa Campaciñas

~

Introduction

Now in its third year, this anthology, *The Good Life in Galicia 2018*, and the Good Life in Galicia competition behind it, began in 2016 as an idea for a competition to encourage people to write about Galicia and raise awareness internationally of this fascinating part of Green Spain. As we are an English-language publisher, the stories had to be in English, and to make it easy, entrants did not have to have lived in Galicia or even to have visited here. These requirements remained the same for the 2018 edition and will continue to apply to the 2019 competition, but in 2017 we added a poetry category, as Galicia, one of the Celtic lands, is a land of poets. Hence again this year there is a plethora of good poetry here.

We were pleased in 2018 to have again had entries from as far afield as Australia and the Orkney Islands, as well as entries in all categories from Galicians.

There were outstanding contest entries in each category, and our judge, Olivia Stowe, had a difficult time choosing her winners. Winner in the fiction category was Michelle Northwood, with her entry "The Witch's Prediction", with its surprise ending. In the nonfiction category, the story "The Man of the Grapes", a story of a family by Galician Vanesa De La Puente Blanco, was the winner. In poetry, the winner for the second year running was Liza Grantham, this year with her amusing poem about having a market stall, "At Market in Antes".

The bulk of this anthology comprises competition entries with the addition of works submitted for inclusion by several local and international authors.

We hope you enjoy this third, brief look at an ancient land, one full of generous people and natural splendours, and agree that there is indeed a lot of good in a life in Galicia.

~

The Magical Pull of Galicia

The Longing

by Dawn Hawkins
(Third place poetry)

It rises like dew on the grass in a morning.
It comes like a glimpse of mountains through the mist.
And when I see a certain shade of green along a valley,
My Galicia, I am longing, for the home I miss . . .

Sometimes it's the sight of seafood on a griddle,
or the ozone when the ocean touches shore.
But when I look, it's beyond the infinite horizon,
My Galician home, the place I'm longing for.

One day when I smelt woodsmoke in the autumn
and found some houses made of stone,
I saw a road that wound through forest.
I thought for one brief moment . . . thought that road might lead
me home.

Today beside a grapevine on a hillside,
I'm drinking wine that tastes of grass and sun.
And far, far below me is a river,
and I know, that when that longing comes,

No matter how good and rich my life is,
when I stand in a land that's not my own,
My heart will hear the music of the bagpipes,
my soul will sing the ancient songs . . . of Galicia my home.

~

The Witch's Prediction

by Michele Northwood

(First place fiction)

Tuesday:

Sally stood beside the coach, her clipboard poised and ready at a forty-five-degree angle, waiting to tick off the members of her tour group as they boarded the bus. This was her first trip to Northern Spain, and even though she had been working as a rep for several years and knew the job inside out, she still found the thrill of being in a new place immensely exciting. On this, the second day of the tour, she felt almost impatient to set off on the day's excursion and was relishing the opportunity of exploring the area, meeting new people, and having the chance to learn new customs and traditions.

The hotel doors abruptly opened wide and her elderly clients began to emerge from the Hotel Sanxenxo in small clusters of six or eight. Despite the tour still being in its infancy, the tourists had already begun to make new acquaintances, forge new friendships, and little 'cliques' were beginning to materialise. These groups were easily recognisable by the amalgam of expressions each assemblage so openly demonstrated as they approached their rep: sleepiness from the late-night partygoers; defeated resignation from those who would much rather have spent the day by the pool and were boarding the coach under duress; devilment from those who always found the funny side of life; and excitement from those who, like Sally, enjoyed the thrill of exploring new domains.

Sally made polite conversation as the excursionists boarded the coach. Then, after she had done the mandatory head count, she headed back to the front of the vehicle. She frantically scanned the long, steep street ahead for a glimpse of Juan, the Galician guide the holiday company had provided her with and whom was frequently becoming a source of exasperation for her.

17

As seemed to be the norm, Juan was late. He should have arrived half an hour ago to greet the guests with Sally, but he was nowhere in sight. As the tourists took their seats and chattered quietly amongst themselves, their rep picked up the microphone to greet her guests officially.

"Good morning everyone! I trust you all had a good night's sleep?" It was not really posed as a question and Sally did not wait for a reply. She was waffling, hoping that the illusive Juan was about to show up. "We will be setting off in just a moment. This morning we will be accompanied by our local tour guide again, who will tell you all about the area."

As some of her clients expressed their surprise that they would not be listening to Sally's mellifluous tones, others continued to chatter amongst themselves in various degrees of excitement.

"So, where's the Galician gigolo this morning?" Mike, one of her more forward clients remarked, smiling knowingly in Sally's direction.

Fortunately, Sally spied her elusive companion ambling towards them.

"There," she replied pan-faced, pointing in her colleague's direction. Mike shrugged and then sat down as Juan came sauntering nonchalantly towards the bus, hands in his pockets as though time were of no importance. He made eye contact and, raising his arm, waved in salutation before breaking into a halfhearted jog. Seconds later, he jumped aboard, flashing his most beguiling smile in her direction.

"*Hola, Guapa!*" He grinned, taking the microphone in one swift movement that involved cupping his right hand over hers in the process and then gently squeezing.

Sally snatched her hand away, reacting as though she had received an electric shock. As simple as that she realised that she had relinquished all control to the handsome, if somewhat irksome, Juan. She had planned to discreetly reprimand his tardiness, but there was a smouldering passion behind his laughing dark-brown eyes that seemed to unwillingly drag Sally magnetically inside, making her incapable of muttering a single intelligible syllable. Knowing that her words of admonishment would almost certainly fall upon deaf ears, she unwittingly sat down, feeling more than a little flustered, something which was totally out of character for her.

"Hello everyone! For those of you who don´t know me, my name is Juan," he began, his singsong, lyrical, Galician dialect echoing around the bus. "And this is Pedro, who will be driving the coach this morning." He pointed in the direction of the bus driver who instantaneously engaged gear and set the coach in motion.

"Today, we have a very exciting tour for you! Our trip this morning is to Cambados," Juan continued, leaning nonchalantly against the back of one of the seats and swaying in rhythm to the motion of the 'Bernardos' bus. He gabbled on, nonstop, as the coach negotiated the steep slope from the hotel down towards the town.

Pedro made a swift turn to the left, and the guests and Sally sat quietly, taking in their surroundings as the coach left the coastal town of Sanxenxo and headed out towards open countryside. They were obediently looking left or right throughout the journey, as Juan virtually ordered them to peer out of the windows at various objects and places of interest while he educated them all on the historical and cultural values of the area.

"Now look left. Can you see the little wooden house on stilts? Yes? Well, in Gallego this is called *un Piorno*, or in Castillano, *un Hórreo*. . . . No, nothing to do with the American biscuits!" He laughed. "These little structures were, and in most cases still are, used to store grain and feed for animals. Now, these were built on stone stilts and the round disc-like stones you can see at the top of each column are there to stop the mice and rats from being able to enter the wooden *Hórreo* . . ."

Sally's tourists expressed their delight and surprise at the information and clicked cameras or mobile phones to capture the raised granary forever, as Juan continued his well-rehearsed speech.

Sally found herself fighting to stay awake. The lilting voice of her coworker, coupled with the gentle rocking of the coach, threatened to lull her to sleep. The night before she had arranged to meet Juan in the hotel reception and they had wandered through to the bar in order to discuss the remaining excursions the Holiday Company had included in their itinerary. Juan, however, had had other plans.

"Let´s get out of here!" he suggested. "We're being watched all the time by your tour group," he complained. "I don´t like it. It's making me feel uncomfortable!"

Sally had to agree. No matter which direction she chanced to glance, someone flashed a knowing smile in her direction, incorrectly assuming that Juan was her boyfriend—or at least a prospective one.

Juan abruptly stood up, grabbed Sally´s elbow, and pulled her to her feet.

"Come on, let's go."

Inadvertently blushing, Sally shuffled away, imagining what her clients would be thinking now!

The couple headed off to Porto Novo, the nearest village, supposedly to discuss the schedule and to have dinner away from the holidaymakers. Juan, who had grown up around these parts, was enthusiastic to show her around.

"This way!" he said striding out towards a rustic establishment called El Vagabundo. The restaurant was full of Galician charm and swarming with locals who battled to be heard over each other; the clatter of cutlery on chinaware, and the vibrant music that echoed around the establishment.

"This place is well known in these parts for its seafood and cider," he explained, greeting and kissing several friends as he sauntered inside. Sally followed behind him, feeling even less inconspicuous than she had in the hotel bar, as Juan's friends looked her up and down, assessing his latest conquest.

A small table was quickly cleared, a second chair was dragged into position, and they were promptly seated, where Juan immediately took control and ordered for both of them.

As they were sipping cider and discussing the itinerary, waiting for their meal, Sally became aware of a tense nervousness that seemed to have mysteriously enveloped the establishment. The room had unexpectedly quietened and an uneasy stillness fell, settling on the diners, enshrouding them with a frisson of fear as they all appeared to be looking in the same direction.

Sally followed their gaze and spied an old woman wearing a shabby, long, black skirt and a faded, dark-red, hooded cape, who was shuffling amongst the tables, apparently looking for someone in particular. Each occupant notably held their breath, and their eyes darted nervously from left to right, as they waited with bated breath for the woman to slowly pass them by. Once out of danger, they eventually exhaled a relieved sigh and began to talk to each other again, tentatively, in whispered overtones, when they were certain they were not the object of the old maid's search.

Sally cringed inwardly and the hair at the nape of her neck stood to attention as she made eye contact with the old woman and realised that the aged crone was heading in her direction.

"Hola chicos, yo soy Juanita y por algunos euros, os puedo decir la fortuna!"

"Do you want your fortune told?" Juan asked, while simultaneously placing Sally's right palm into Juanita's hand and planting a few coins in the other.

"Well, I . . ."

"Esto es muy interesante . . ." The witch began as Juan translated.

"She says this is very interesting. . . . You will have a very long life. . . . You will never be very rich, but you will have a lot of children."

Sally snorted, feeling more than a little embarrassed. She momentarily wished she were back in the hotel bar, being stared at by her tour group, rather than a restaurant full of complete strangers who, like her guests, were glancing intermittently over in her direction.

"Huh! That could apply to basically everyone!" Sally retorted.

The old maid's eyes narrowed, making Sally wonder if she had been understood.

"She says that you are new here and you are in for a big surprise. You will fall in love!" Juan said, his dark eyes dancing with delight. "And you will make Galicia your home!"

"Yeah, right, well, that's enough of that!" Sally snatched her hand away from the witch. She was unsure if Juan was actually translating the crone's words, or if he was amusing himself and playing with her, but either way, she was really starting to feel uncomfortable.

The old woman's eyes narrowed. She smiled slyly in Sally's direction whilst simultaneously pocketing the coins inside her diaphanous gown.

"*Suerte!*" she whispered and then shuffled out of the restaurant.

* * * *

The hissing and spitting of the coach brakes coming to a gradual stop forced Sally back to the present and she eyed the coastal village of Cambados for the first time.

"Follow me! Follow me!" Juan shouted, jumping from the bus and striding out in the direction of the main square. The holidaymakers hastily gathered their belongings together and set off in pursuit of their illusive guide.

Sally brought up the rear, and when she finally caught up with the rest of her group, Juan had come to a stop. The assemblage was clustering around him, dabbing their damp foreheads with handkerchiefs, rubbing tired limbs caused by the brisk walk, or rooting in their bags for bottles of water. Juan pointed to a Neoclassical building and began his well-rehearsed speech.

"Oh, dear!" Mike whispered conspiratorially in Sally's ear. "I hope this isn´t going to be another ABC tour!"

"What do you mean?"

"A, B, C . . . Another Bloody Church!" He quipped.

Sally tried to stifle her laughter as Juan flashed an angry look in their direction.

"OK, so, we are standing in La Plaza de Fefiñans," Juan continued. "Here, to my left is the church of San Benito, or in Gallego, La Igrexa de San Bieito. It was built approximately in the fifteenth century, and it was remodelled in the seventeenth century. The outside shows both the Neoclassical and Baroque styles, whereas the inside of the church is in a Gothic style . . ."

As Juan continued his spiel, two older women fought their way through the crowd and shuffled towards Sally.

"Where can we get a cream tea?" one of them asked.

"I beg your pardon?"

"We don´t want to listen to the rest of this. We want to sit down," they explained. "Can you recommend the best place to get a cream tea?"

"Err . . . Devon?" Sally replied, pan-faced. "There´s nothing like that around here, I'm afraid. We are in Spain, you know."

The women sniffed in annoyance and Sally knew she had just blown any chances of an end-of-tour tip from them.

"There are a couple of bars over there," she said. "You should be able to get a cup of tea or coffee and maybe a tapa, or a small cake, but scones and clotted cream are definitely out of the question, I'm afraid," she said, with a smile.

Slightly more appeased, the ladies wandered off in the direction of the establishments, suddenly veering swiftly to the left when they realised that the bar they were approaching had been commandeered by a group of young, Spanish hippies who seemed contented to merely sit around the bars smoking, drinking, and chatting.

Juan's dulcet tones honed in on Sally's auditory senses once again.

". . . .On the right we can see the Palace of Fefiñanes. It was here that . . . ."

As the plethora of information continued to flow effortlessly from her colleague's mouth, Sally looked towards the impressive edifice, with its crumbling coat of arms, and breathed in the atmosphere with a sigh of deep contentment. Equating herself to a time traveller, she became momentarily disengaged from reality. For a fleeting moment she perceived that she was simultaneously trapped between two diverging time/space continuums: two contradictory interposed dimensions, both interlaced with each other, yet one was totally unconscious of the other's existence.

The square's architecture cried out of ancient times, of battles won and lost, of forbidden love and forgotten gentry, all preposterously overlaid by a myriad of modern-day tourists with floppy sun hats, socks, and sandals. Interlaced with the tourists, the group of young Spanish hippies, dressed in day-glow colours, broke into song accompanied by a lone Spanish guitar, totally oblivious to their ancestral past.

Sally headily drank in the atmosphere. There was a certain magic about Galicia that both captivated and intrigued her.

". . . Now, if you'll follow me, we can take a short tour inside the impressive bodega of Fefiñanes, where their wine and sherry, or Jerez, is stored in huge wooden barrels." Juan strode towards the bodega as the tourists expressed their delight, shuffled together and blindly followed their guide, evoking in Sally images of herded sheep.

* * * *

Later, as the last stragglers wandered back outside, Juan left the tourists to their own devices. Taking a forceful hold of Sally's elbow, he steered her away.

"Come, let's go for a drink," he said, pointing to one of the bars Sally had previously indicated to her two female clients.

"No, I want to look in the little shop and get a souvenir," she replied, casually removing his hand.

Juan shrugged nonchalantly.

"*Vale, Bonita,*" he said and immediately sauntered over towards the group of hippies.

Sally wandered across the square to a little gift shop laden with enticing trinkets to attract the passing trade. T-shirts, key rings, jewellery, and ornaments cluttered the walls and shelves outside the establishment in a bid to allure the eyes, entice the tourists, and hopefully open their wallets.

Sally traversed the entrance, and her gaze fell on a shelf of ornaments. Each one was in the form of a witch holding a short message: something that, even with her limited Spanish, she was able to decipher. '*La bruja de la suerte*', the good luck witch, and '*la bruja de la salud*', the witch of good health. She chose one carrying a backpack, surmising that it was the lucky witch of travel, which seemed appropriately apt for her and would also remind her of her encounter with the crone the night before.

24

At the counter the aged shop assistant smiled and took the ornament from Sally's hands.

"Maybe this not the witch for you," she said, narrowing her eyes and fixing her with a piercing expression. "I think, for you, the witch of Love."

Sally gasped. Once again, visions of the encounter with the old woman in Porto Novo swam before her and she was more than a little perturbed by the coincidence. She shivered involuntarily, endeavouring to dismiss the thought from her mind.

"No, *Gracias*. Just this one please."

The shop assistant shrugged, muttering something under her breath, obviously a little peeved that her advice was not being heeded.

Sally wandered out into the square again and Juan appeared magically by her side.

"Time to get these tourists back to the hotel," he said, squeezing her arm. "Everyone back to the coach!" he yelled, immediately striding off, leaving Sally and the stragglers to follow swiftly in his wake.

* * * *

Wednesday:

"Good morning people!" Juan began. "Today, we are going to the Valdeamor bodega, where we will be able to sample some of Galicia's most famous wine, called Albariño. Now, Alba comes from the Latin word 'Albar' and means 'white,' so I suppose you can all guess what type of wine we will be drinking this afternoon. Yes?"

The transfixed members of the group either muttered or shouted their answers in various modes of enthusiasm while Juan, as usual, continued regardless.

"Yes, that's correct, white wine! This type of grape is grown in the Rias Baixas," or "The Low Rivers," he explained. "And the bodega is situated in the centre of the Rias Baixas area, so we are sure to see a large quantity of vineyards dotted around the countryside during our excursion today."

Half an hour later, the coach pulled onto the forecourt of the Valdeamor bodega. The tourists craned their necks over the seats to view the impressive building painted in a dusky pink hew that seemed a little faded and tired with age, weatherworn from being battered by the cold Galician winter wind and rain.

"Follow me, please!" Juan shouted energetically as he jumped athletically off the bus and immediately strode off towards the main entrance. Sally watched him as he shook hands with the proprietor and disappeared inside, quickly followed by the most interested, or athletic, members of her group.

The party was herded down into the bowels of the building as an employee explained the wine-making procedure in great detail, from the arrival of the grapes and destalking procedure, to the storage and fermentation process in huge metal vats. Finally, the group was taken to witness the bottling and labelling of the Albariño wine.

Suitably impressed, they were later escorted back upstairs into a long room that housed a resplendent, elongated, heavy, wooden table with a host of matching antique chairs around it. At least they seemed antique to Sally's novice eyes. At one end of the table, tall, thin glasses of Albariño sat on a silver tray, waiting to be sipped and savoured, accompanied by various platters of cubed cheese that were strategically placed along the length of the table.

Each visitor took a glass and chose a seat. Sally joined in and sniffed the dramatic aromatic intensity, reminding her of nectarines and beeswax, honeysuckle and oranges. She sipped it tentatively and was surprised by the host of flavours that bombarded her taste buds. Juan plonked himself next to her, grinning slightly as she sipped the wine.

"Cheers, *salud,*" he said, clinking glasses. "It's good, no?"

Sally nodded and then smiled in the direction of the proprietor, who stood quietly to one side, surveying the group with rapt attention. From his isolated position, he returned Sally's smile and perused the group, waiting confidently for praise regarding his lifetime's work. Sally cringed as some of her clients screwed up their faces and professed the wine to be too dry for their taste. Others, however, were delighted with the acidic, refreshing citrus flavour and subtle saltiness.

As the guests wandered around the entrance, examining the variety of bottles and wooden cases available for purchase, the proprietor caught the two reps together.

"This is on the house," he said, pushing a bottle of Albariño into Sally's hands. "It is a great choice of wine for a wedding. You should keep that in mind!"

Sally blushed as Juan grinned and some of the tourists giggled; several slightly inebriated from the wine.

* * * *

Thursday:

Sally spent the day accompanying her group as they toured Santiago de Compostela in the pouring rain. By the time they had wandered through the streets, joined the queue inside the cathedral, and kissed the stone at the Apostle James's feet, they were exhausted, dishevelled, and soaking wet. Sally surveyed them with a hint of amusement. They sported a variety of waterproof jackets and brightly coloured rain ponchos, most of which had been hasty impulsive buys when the heavens had opened and the deluge had begun. They stood huddled together, shivering with cold under the impressive but presently inactive botafumeiro, the huge old silver incense burner hanging from the vaulted ceiling and designed in such large proportions to mask the unpleasant smell medieval pilgrims, reminding Sally of a collection of broken umbrellas as the coloured plastic hung down limply, dripping water all over the cathedral floor.

Later, as they took their places in the coach and settled down for the drive back to Sanxenxo, a satisfied ambience settled on the travellers. Juan's vast knowledge of Santiago and the cathedral, coupled with his charismatic charm, not to mention the rain, had made the excursion unforgettable for them all. He had even persuaded a travelling band of "Tunas"—small groups of university musicians who sang and played instruments to collect funds for their studies—to board the bus and serenade the tourists.

By the end of the day, Sally felt strangely content, knowing that Juan had easily succeeded in winning the respect of the male tourists and the hearts of most of the ladies, with his charismatic smile and easygoing manner.

* * * *

Friday:

The trip to La Coruña turned into a nightmarish experience for Sally when two of her guests, Mike and his wife, wandered off, became disorientated, and failed to return to the coach on time. Forced to stay behind while Juan continued with the rest of the group to the next place of interest, she was more than a little relieved when the errant couple finally appeared forty minutes later.

"Sorry, sorry! We got completely lost!" they apologised in unison.

"Thank you for waiting, we knew you wouldn't go without us!" Mike grinned sheepishly.

"But now we've made you have to split up from your boyfriend," his wife added.

"He's not my boyfriend!" Sally replied vehemently. The couple smiled smugly, refusing to believe it and tick-tacked between themselves as she bundled them in a taxi and then clambered into the front seat to give the driver directions.

When they finally managed to catch up with the others, Sally discovered that another client had fallen ill on the steps of La Torre de Hercules. Juan was phoning for an ambulance and gently patting the woman's hand as a small group of onlookers stood around, taking in the situation, concerned about their travelling companion's well-being.

"What's happened?" Sally asked, alarmed.

"She just collapsed," Juan replied, abruptly turning away to talk to the emergency services on his mobile phone.

Sally looked at the woman in concern.

"Don't worry, dear, I just felt a little faint," the elderly woman explained, as she sensed Sally's concern. "Juan has been great. He's never left my side. You've got a good one there."

Sally smiled. It seemed pointless trying to deny, yet again, that there was a romantic relationship between the two of them. The woman continued to look at her with a knowing smile.

"He really likes you, you know. I can tell."

* * * *

Saturday:

The following day, the group headed out to visit the quaint fishing village of Combarro, with its winding narrow streets juxtaposed by its modern port, which sported an amalgam of stylish bars and restaurants. Half of the tour group had chosen to remain in the bars rather than negotiate the precarious wooden stairs built over the original mounds of rocks, which led to a rabbit warren of narrow streets.

Sally had joined the most adventurous tourists and traversed the whimsically paved caminos. One of her clients, the lady who had become ill the day before, came out of one of the tiny gift shops and handed Sally a paper bag.

"Here, Sally, this is for you. It´s just a little something to say thank you for all your help the other day," she explained.

"Oh, there was no need to do this", Sally said, tearing the package open. She stared incredulously at the ornament: The witch of love. "Thank you," she muttered, feeling herself redden.

"Like I said the other day, Juan's a good catch and he really likes you. Who knows, maybe with the help of this witch, both your destinies will be sealed forever".

* * * *

Sunday:

As the week finally drew to a close, Sally stood on the terrace of the Hotel Sanxenxo, drinking in her last view of the town. Looking out at the crystal-blue sea swirling and undulating towards the shore, she spied La Madama de Silgar, a statue with a snail-like quality, poised on a rock out at sea, holding a conch shell in her hands: a picture of sereneness. Sally could have quite easily stayed there forever.

Later, at the airport, as she stood beside the coach, her clipboard poised and ready at a forty-five-degree angle, waiting to tick off the members of her tour group and escort them into the departures terminal, she looked around at the scenery before her.

It was so beautiful here, everything seemed tinged with magic. Even the flora seemed different from home in England. It was richer, greener, somehow more vibrant and alive. In her mind, she replayed the events of the past week. Images of Juan flashed intermittently through her memories. His patience as he explained the history and culture of this beautiful area, the way he brought everything to life. His wicked charm, his carefree manner, and his idiosyncrasies made her smile. Then, without warning, the image of the witch and her words came back to haunt Sally yet again.

"You'll fall in love. You'll make Galicia your home."

Sally finally realised that she would have to admit the truth: The crone's prediction had come true. Unbelievably, she had fallen in love, but not with Juan, although he would always be a good friend. No, she had fallen head over heels in love with Galicia. She would have to leave this green and pleasant land in order to fulfil her contract, but she also knew that she would return, and the next time, she would definitely not be leaving again!

~

In Pursuit of a Dream

by Liza Grantham
(Second place non fiction)

Our decision to move to Galicia came about rather suddenly. For the last five years we had been living in the Canary Islands, the Spanish archipelago in the Atlantic Ocean to the west of Morocco. Our apartment in Las Palmas, Gran Canaria, was situated in the old quarter of the city, surrounded by charming examples of colonial architecture and steeped in ancient history and local tradition. Our income enabled us to live comfortably, enjoying the rich variety of culture and cuisine the island had to offer, and, thanks to the temperate climate, weekends could be spent on the beach at almost any time of the year.

To begin with, the lifestyle suited us well, but over time we were becoming increasingly discontented: year upon year of heat and humidity was stifling; the noise and pollution of the city was oppressive; apartment living felt like imprisonment; even the weekend routine of bars and beaches seemed mundane—in short, Gran Canaria was rapidly losing its appeal. We began to enjoy spending holidays off the island, often on the Spanish peninsula, as flights were reasonable due to our status as residents.

Our next destination was to be Galicia. We were drawn by a desire to experience the region's cultural tradition of pipe music, its breathtaking verdant landscapes, its excellent gastronomic reputation, and its ancient background of pilgrimage and mysticism. Whilst browsing for places of cultural interest, I came across news of a Celtic music festival, the Festival do Mundo Celto, in the town of Ortigueira, on the north coast of the province of A Coruña. A campsite close to the beach, staged musical performances by famous artists in the nearby town, impromptu sessions in the streets by local bands of pipers, or *gaiteros*—all completely free! This sounded an idyllic way to escape the stress and tedium of the island.

* * * *

The festival campsite lay at the foot of a vast expanse of pine forest, above a stretch of dunes framing the white sands of Playa de Morouzos, on the tranquil estuary of the Ria de Santa Marta de Ortigueira. We were immediately enchanted by the beauty of the surrounding countryside and uplifted by the once-familiar sight of field and forest stretching out for miles—such a contrast to the arid volcanic scrubland sparsely dotted with cactus and palm. To the south was the marine town of Ortigueira, where the legacies of its ancestors—the Celts, the Romans, and the Spanish monarchs—can still be seen: the primitive mound, or *castro*, on which the town stands; the once-haughty fortification of el Chan da Torre, now an overgrown ruin; the noble squares, or *plazas*, with their proud stone fountains overlooked by windowed balconies; the hidden corners and walkways where time seems to stand still. We spent our afternoons relaxing in the plazas, enjoying the carefree atmosphere and the sound of *gaiteros* performing their traditional songs.

As we strolled through the town on our final afternoon, my husband, Gary, drew my attention to the window of an estate agency. Many of the properties were ancient stone houses in remote countryside.

"Aren't they gorgeous?" I sighed. "So old, so full of character, so . . ."

"But look at the *prices!*" interrupted Gary. "It's unbelievable!"

He was right. Some of the properties were on sale for as little as twelve thousand euros.

"My God," he exclaimed. "We could buy one outright!"

"We could fly out every holiday—you know, a sort of restoration project!" I gabbled excitedly. "Eventually, we could live here!"

"We'd grow our own vegetables," said Gary. "And I could tend pigs."

The image of a welly-clad husband squelching about in a pigpen was hilarious. I dissolved into laughter.

Drawn by the prospect of refreshment and a seat in the shade, we moved on. We settled at a table on the corner of the main square and chatted idly over our beers, pausing from time to time to listen to the passing pipe bands. Now and again our conversation drifted back to those lovely old stone houses and how wonderful it would be to buy one. Looking back on that hazy summer afternoon, it's hard to recall how or when we decided that what had started as a flight of fancy could actually be something achievable, but by nightfall, our faces aglow from the warmth of our campfire, not to mention a glass or two of red wine, we drank to a future in rural Galicia. A moment of fantasy was about to become the pursuit of a dream.

* * * *

Back in Las Palmas, we explored websites advertising houses for sale in Galicia, and eventually came upon one we thought might meet our needs. Mark Adkinson was an English estate agent who had lived in Galicia for over thirty years. He spoke fluent Spanish and Galician and had extensive firsthand knowledge of the rural areas of Lugo Province. We made contact by telephone to gain a personal impression of the man we might be dealing with and to ask a few basic questions about what was involved. Reassured by our initial conversation, we eagerly set about our search.

The website offered a variety of rural properties in the provinces of Lugo, Pontevedra, and A Coruña, ranging from tiny rustic houses to luxurious, stately homes. So many of the houses were within our price range, each with its own unique character and charm: a quaint little mill house beside a fast-flowing stream; a vine covered cottage nestled into the side of a valley; a huge rambling farmhouse surrounded by courtyards, enclosed within high stone walls—it was incredible to think that any of these could be ours. In reality, however, the houses were in varying states of disrepair, from slightly dilapidated to completely ruinous—no matter how pretty or charming they might appear, this was clearly not a time for romanticism.

Pushing sentimentality aside, we drew up a sensible set of criteria. The house would need to have water and electricity. The walls and roof must be basically sound. It must have land attached, at the very least enough for a decent vegetable garden and a few chickens. It would stand on its own, with no close neighbours. Once we'd applied our criteria, the shortlist was surprisingly small. We examined photographs to select the houses we felt had character and potential.

Our final choice rested on a house in a remote situation, twenty kilometres northwest of the city of Lugo. It stood alone on a triangular slope of land at the side of a barely used road, a hundred metres from its nearest neighbour. From the photographs it was clear that the house had long been untended, but its basic structure appeared sound, and it had supplies of water and electricity. Upstairs was a bathroom and three small bedrooms. Downstairs, apart from the kitchen, the rest was nothing but animal pens, offering great potential to create a personalised living space. We arranged to fly out for a viewing at the beginning of November.

* * * *

From the roadside the house appeared bleak, almost forbidding. It was immediately apparent that it had deteriorated considerably since the photographs had been taken and would need some basic structural attention. The slate roof now sank slightly inwards, and on an outbuilding to the side an area of stone wall had collapsed. Only a few panes of glass remained in the windows and most of the shutters had fallen from rusty hinges or rotted away. Mark pushed open the door and a chilly draught welcomed us as we entered a narrow entrance passage littered with leaves. Through a door to the right was a dingy kitchen with a typical wood-burning stove, or *cociña*, yielding sadly to rust. Beneath the broken window was a bare concrete sink, and a small wooden dresser stood in the far corner. Mark assured us that the stove would still be in working order and suggested that a good scrub and a few coats of paint would be all it would take to transform this into a homely space for cooking and eating. I tried to imagine myself untying my apron after a morning of baking and pickling, with chickens pecking around the doorstep and the smell of freshly made bread in the air.

Opposite the kitchen an open doorway led into a windowless room sectioned into pig pens. Gary wondered if the odour of muck and swill had drifted into the kitchen during mealtimes. With the ugly concrete walls and feed troughs removed, I thought it would be ideal as a storeroom for garden tools, waterproofs and wellies.

At the end of the passage another door opened into an expanse of animal pens, with earthen floors still strewn with straw. To the side, an archway led into a smaller stable, which housed a traditional stone-built bread oven. Beyond the pens, a low barn spanned the breadth of the house, overlooking the land to the rear. We recognised at once the enormous scope for imaginative restoration, a blank canvas on which to design the home of our dreams. Mark saw the potential for knocking down the central area to create an inner courtyard; I pictured a spacious dining area and a sunny lounge overlooking vegetable patches beyond; Gary imagined removing the walls of the stable, leaving a covered patio area for bread-oven barbecues on summer nights. All of our ideas were feasible, but they would involve a considerable investment of time and money. By now our heads were reeling as our sums waged war on our aspirations.

Through the final door a narrow wooden staircase led up to a bare landing, with windows overlooking the front and side of the house, and pleasant views of fields and farmhouses beyond. A constant drip from the ceiling had left a patch of damp, rotting floorboards and indicated that the roof was in need of urgent repair. Doors on two sides opened into a tiny bathroom and three small bedrooms, in the second of which a bare electrical wire sizzled menacingly. In contrast to my earlier feelings, I suddenly sensed an inexplicable uneasiness, an almost eerie sensation, as though something was warning us away. I quickly pulled myself together, reasoning that this was nonsensical and merely a reaction to the cold and dismal atmosphere of a house abandoned for years.

Back outside, it had begun to drizzle, but I soon recovered my cheerful optimism as I surveyed our surroundings.

In front of the house stood a typical Galician grain store, or *horreo*, a log store and a cluster of apple and pear trees. To the rear a sizeable area of land stretched down to two magnificent chestnut trees.

Our tour completed, we now faced a huge dilemma. We realised that it would be a long and costly process to restore the house to a basic level of comfort before we could even *begin* to think about embarking on more ambitious projects—it could be years before we were finally able to live there. On the other hand, although we would have to continue working on the island longer than we'd originally hoped, we'd be able to put aside plenty of money to fund our venture—the eventual outcome would make the sacrifice worthwhile. Of course, there was no need to decide there and then—we could have taken as much time as we wanted to discuss our options. Somehow, though, discussion didn't even occur to us—caught up in a fog of excitement and enthusiasm, our hearts were ruling our heads. Impulsively, we made an offer.

* * * *

A week passed and we received no news. Gary rang to find out what was causing the delay. Mark explained that the house had been bequeathed to nine siblings, all of whom first had to be contacted and would then have to discuss our offer. It could take another week. The next week passed and we heard nothing more. Anxiously, I urged Gary to ring again.

"Eight have agreed, but there's a problem with number nine," Mark told him.

"Is he holding out for the full asking price?"

"No, it's not your offer that's the problem. There's a bit of a family politics thing going on. Seems that the eldest gets ten grand more than the others; this fella's not happy about it."

"What now, then?"

"The others are threatening to sue him, so chances are he'll come round. Just have to be patient. I'll let you know as soon as I hear something."

I was becoming despondent, and doubts were beginning to nag at the back of my mind. Perhaps fate was intervening, steering us away with a protective arm? Then, in the first week of December, a month since our visit, we received a call: number nine had finally given in! With the Christmas holidays approaching, the timing was ideal. A mutually convenient date was agreed and Mark contacted the *notario* to arrange an appointment for the signing. Suddenly, all doubts were dispelled.

We arranged to fly out the day after Boxing Day to complete the purchase, returning on New Year's Eve. The house became known to us as *os Castaneiros*, the Chestnut Trees, and with typical enthusiasm, we began to draw up our plans for its restoration. The waiting was unbearable, but our planning kept us busy for the next three weeks. Even Christmas Day held little significance for us that year. Our thoughts were on nothing but returning to Lugo. Little did we realise that our dream was about to turn to dust.

* * * *

On December 30th, just after noon, we arrived at the *notario*'s premises, situated in an office block above a small shopping mall on Rúa da Raiña, in the centre of Lugo. Eight of the family were already assembled, all keen to convert their crumbling inheritance into cash. In turn, they introduced themselves and explained that they were waiting for the ninth member, Jesus, to complete the group. Mark frowned on hearing the name—this was the man who'd initially refused to sell.

By twenty minutes past twelve he had still not arrived. Mark was anxious, and the family themselves were beginning to show signs of concern. I still felt confident that he'd appear, reasoning that the roads might be busier than usual due to the impending bank holiday. At twelve thirty, Mark spoke to the family and one of the women produced a mobile phone. Seconds later her expression grew serious and it was clear that something was wrong. When the call ended, she spoke to the others. Raised voices spoke rapidly in Galician. Mark was summoned over, then returned to us, shaking his head in stunned disbelief. He explained:

"He's working on an oil tanker off the coast of Vigo. His drill's broken and he can't leave until he's finished the job. I'm really sorry folks, the sale won't be going ahead today."

Gary and I looked at one another, incredulous. Here we were in the middle of Lugo, with a shoulder bag stuffed full of bundles of money and due to fly home the next day. Everything suddenly seemed surreal. I felt like an observer, powerless to alter the cruel chain of events that was unravelling before me. I remained speechless, struggling to make sense of our situation. Gary was determined that our mission would not be thwarted.

"How about tomorrow?" he suggested. "If we were finished by three o'clock we'd still be in time for our flight."

Mark went inside to see if it would be possible to reschedule the appointment. He returned with good news. The office was due to close at one o'clock for the New Year holiday, but if we began at twelve thirty, the *notario*, most generously, was prepared to stay until two; there would be adequate time to complete the sale. Everyone was satisfied with this arrangement and it seemed that the problem might yet be resolved. All that remained was to contact Jesus a second time to put forward the proposal. This time Mark rang. His voice soon became agitated, then angry. The call ended abruptly.

"Bastard hung up," he grunted.

The following day we returned to Gran Canaria, more than a thousand euros out of pocket, all for the pursuit of a dream.

Author's Note:

We returned to Galicia the following April to look at another property. This time the sale went ahead successfully— only three days after the viewing! We have lived there happily for seven years, growing vegetables and raising chickens. Our thanks go to Mark Adkinson, of www.galicianrustic.com.

~

The Galician countryside with terraced vineyards and fincas.
Photo by J. P. Vincent

The Man Who Captures Time

by Adrian Casanova
(Third place fiction)

Beauty

>   Noun UK /'bju: ti/ US/'bju ti/ [no plural]
>   The quality of being beautiful from a subjective point of
view.

"Beauty" murmured the pilot flying above Riberia Sacra

The sun is still sleeping at these coordinates. It is cold despite being summer. Two shadows walk through the fog. They are going to the summit, the rock tower, to see the deep river Lor valley, tributary of the Sil. They are going up, expelling their breath like a steam locomotive following invisible rails. At this moment, pine needles have water pearls.

How did this story begin?

Our man has a name, obviously. He is Gundræd, the Dane. His origin implies a ~~great~~ long story. Let's sum up! Sometimes life hits our lives with ferocity. When all was lost, he used a glass compass to look for new ways. Toward unknown places, he became a pilgrim twelve years ago. What was his fuel? Sadness.

On this journey, a lot of stories and anecdotes were merged, like a Russian doll. The foremost ones:

The Creek

His feet were covered by monstrous blisters near the end of Santiago's Winter Way. He strayed off the path and found a fresh creek, covered by alder tree leaves. Coins of light made a brilliant effect that could recall a kaleidoscope. Into the creek, laughter. A woman, pilgrim as well, refreshing her painful feet.

The kaleidoscopic light caressed her, her smile caressed him. Érika.

Gundræd had always loved beauty, and unlike other people, he was, and is (nowadays), looking for it too. "We are our minds", he thought in Finisterra's sunset. If our memory someday closes down. . . . Moreover, our memories are not made in marble. They are edited from time to time and time erodes memories too.

"One way to capture time, purely and forever, is by means of photography". He took his camera and pointed at the orange horizon while the sea wind swelled his shirt. Fisterra, the end of all paths.

—Well, well, well. Reduce film speed until ISO 100; reduce shutter speed and aperture. Finally, don't breathe. Shoot!

The most beautiful sunset that he had ever seen was captured.

The Last Train

When you walk a long way there is a one-way ticket. Is there really a return?

Gundræd felt a strong pressure in his chest. Kilometre by kilometre this pressure grew. Without life's way, again. The train went to Monforte, after he would change train at this railway station to go to Madrid. Finally, a flight to Denmark.

Past Ourense, the train converts into a boat, levitating over the Miño and afterwards, over its mighty tributary the Sil River. There is the blue river, the green walls and a blue corridor, our sky.

From the platform, he watched his the train leaving. His hands trembled.

Denmark

—This is too strange. —The fisherman puts a postcard on the wooden table. By the sea, he smokes a cigarette.

—Four people died in the accident, but only three were in the car. You should remember this fact.

—You're right. I agree, my friend. —The fisherman feels a tear skateboarding down his tanned face.

A boat over the Baltic Sea, two fishermen in the boat, a postcard, with the last train wagon leaving the station, on the table.

The Call

—Are you Gundræd Axelsen?
—Yes, I am.
—I am calling you from the hospital . . .

Castaway in Paradise
(as Lois Pereiro would say)

—Are you looking for a job here?
Gundræd nodded repeatedly.
—What would the reason be to hire the strongest man for a hard job? Hahahahaha! Come with me!

Zillions of grapes are waiting for thousands of hired hands, families, and friends on terraced vineyards with elevated slopes. The green tones retreat with autumnal colours from oaks, chestnut trees, cork oaks, and vineyards. A gift for our eyes, whose eyelashes have sweaty dewdrops.

"Shit! I forgot my ice axe", with a bit of humour. So necessary.

From time to time, he took a deep breath, without thinking. During a short moment, he feels like one more piece of this landscape, only of this. Finally, he goes up again with a box full of grapes and, unlike Sisyphus, he reaches the summit.

The last day of the grape harvest of the year has a brushstroke of melancholia, erased with beer toasts with his hired hand colleagues. This job brings people together, once in a while converting job colleagues into friends. Drunk he writes on a napkin:

There is no sea,
here.
I can't navigate

too far.
But I can try
to reach the sky.
Opening its gate.

—Next step, chestnuts!!!
—Mushrooms!
—Cheers!!!

A long time ago, someone told me about a strange emotion. Where? Maybe in a canteen. I remember! She was a job colleague at a steel factory, Karen. She had been on the beach with her grandson last weekend. He was playing happily with other children. She was only seeing the horizon and listening. Finally, they had come home at night.

—Wow! Then? —I asked sarcastically.
—Nothing special.
—I don't understand well. Are you drunk?—More sarcastically.
—For an ephemeral moment, I felt very special with nothing special. It's difficult to describe with the words that I know. It was beauty.
—Beauty . . .
Beauty, beauty...this word sounds like an echo from the valley, from the past. Among colleagues toasting with the colourful views. Suddenly, he feels a strange emotion. Surely, nothing special . . .
—Heeeeeey! Your napkin-poem is flying!
—Hahahahahaha!
—Fuck! —He runs after it.
The napkin moves away, harmonically, until it is trapped by an oak branch. One more leaf in the family. He feels a strange emotion, surely nothing special . . .
. . . He felt special with nothing special.

Nightmare

A hundred people, Gundræd among them, are on the hard shoulder. They are fighting against the forest fire, again. It shall not pass! This road is the last but one border. They are volunteers. Forest firefighters work frenetically to save a hamlet near the forest. The hot wind is whipping them. It is raining ashes, which before were vegetation. The night sky has an orange aurora borealis, or forestalis.

—Shiiit! Behind us!

A new fire is born on the other side of the road.

—Retreat, retreat!

—The hamlet!

During a time, there is a chaos. Gundræd sees, exhausted, sirens, hunted people, dark smoke, melted asphalt. People seem like painted Picts due to the ashes and smoke. Some people fight unarmed against the new fire. Sharply, a ray falls out. Over the smoke, black clouds begin to shoot water artillery.

—Now, now! The hamlet. We can save it!

It is raining very heavily. The fire beast calms down and waits for its death. Nevertheless, the fight continues until daybreak.

That forest is now ash. Where is the forest life? In a spring photo on the cork panel of Gundræd's house.

The Beauty

There are a lot of stories about Gundræd, the pilgrim Dane. Some legends too. In genuine bars, on the land with a sickle and a hoe, at the Paradise Festival and other intense parties, learning Galician, but especially walking with his camera and friendly dog. "Looking for Beauty", he said.

I speak in the past, but don't worry dear reader. He lives. He has just disappeared since last month, walking through the chromatic mountains, with Elm, the dog. Of course, with his camera.

The man and the dog, on the rock summit. The daybreak says "Good morning" to them. He hears something. . . . Suddenly, Gundræd sees it! It is nothing special, but special. He takes the camera and points it. He is trembling, very nervous. He sets up the tripod quickly.

—Come on—whispered Gundræd.

Camera parameters perfectly adjusted, his breathing stops. His chest may burst with his heartbeats. The camera shoots.

Stick your photo here

He feels very special . . .
       . . . with nothing special.
      ~

Rocio's Return
by Fiona Cowan

Rocio clutched the armrests of her seat as the plane began its descent into Santiago de Compostela airport. As usual, the plane was busy with tourists, including several pilgrims, she guessed, judging by their footwear. Although she had grown up in Galicia, she had never even remotely considered doing the Camino. Every time she saw the *peregrinos* walk past her Grandparents' house she was grateful that she didn't have to face the bedbugs in the *albergue,* pilgrim hostel, beds or the mosquitos that attacked by day throughout the humid season. Some people loved the experience and gained from it, but she preferred home comforts, and now she was coming home.

She had not been able to find work anywhere in Galicia despite having both a good degree and a masters behind her. She had opted to study English and she had benefitted greatly from her father marrying his English teacher while she was at high school, or the 'instituto.' as she still called it. She loved her stepmother dearly and often joked that her father had married a woman who was her friend before she was her father's girlfriend. Her own mother had developed presenile dementia, and the costs of her care in the residencia had been crippling for the family. Sometime after her mum passed away her father began learning English and Rocio was able to matchmake for her dad, Guillermo.

Fast forward a few years and she felt her new family was both secure and prospering. Her grandparents still sold produce in the market, but she knew it was just tradition to sell their crops in that manner and that the income was not the real driver. When she could find no job a few years ago she offered to help them out but quickly realised there could be no wage. Galicia was both fertile and fruitful, but nobody could become rich selling grelos, turnip tops, and chestnuts.

So, her only option was to fly the nest and head for the UK. She had found an agency that placed her in a small

47

company producing multimedia products across a range of service areas, and although she initially was only translating text into Spanish, she soon progressed and found herself involved in dubbing sound clips into Spanish. It had amused her greatly to hear her voice being used to make a safety announcement at the regional airport as she waited in line during a previous trip home.

On this visit she was getting a bit nervous about her future plans. The arrival of Brexit had made all European immigrant workers worried about their job status in the UK, but for Rocio it was worse. So many of the projects she had been working on were EU related and she already knew that her company were finding it hard to secure new business. The agency had declined to renew her six-month contract last month, so she was assuming things would become very temporary. This wasn't in her career plan, but to be honest, if she had come up with a career plan, she should have buckled down and studied for her *oposiciones*—the government-run exams that all public service workers needed to pass. For each attempt they paid five hundred euros and were still not guaranteed a job. She could have used her English to teach, but there were no jobs in public education and all the private schools preferred native-English speakers.

So, a holiday at home was in order, but she had decided not to tell her family her concerns until she could find something else first. Her worries about the future could only be helped by a week in Galicia among the best beaches, the most delicious food, and, yes, even among the tourists who were at every local beauty spot trying to read signs in the Galician language rather even than Spanish! It was rather an interesting policy to make interpretation boards available in the local language while the content was intended for tourists who visited the area. She smiled as she remembered a German colleague who was out of the office when a local council e-mailed to ask for an urgent sign telling people to be aware of a dangerous surface. Sadly, the sign was printed with the exact German text of his out-of-office e-mail proclaiming that he would attend to the matter on his return. Poor Franz—his contract had already been terminated and Rocio felt she could be next.

The arrival was smooth and, being five minutes early, she had to endure another in-flight announcement of propaganda celebrating the early arrival with cheering and clapping. But soon enough she was back on terra firma, smelling the air like a puppy. To be honest it was mostly aviation fuel, but soon enough she would smell and taste the salty tang of the Ria and breathe again the clean air, even if it was so humid she already felt her skin prickle with moisture. It was going to be warm!

Her dad was waiting at the self-opening door, and Sandra, her stepmother, was beside him, holding back a little to let Guille hug his daughter before she did. When Sandra gave the traditional *dous bicos,* two cheek kisses, and went to hug her, Rocio called out in excitement.

"Sandra! What are you hiding under that tunic?" Delight surprised Rocio that she might be getting ready to become a big sister. She looked questioningly at her dad and he nodded that, yes, Sandra was *embarasada* (pregnant), but on this occasion she also looked a bit embarrassed, as if there was something vaguely improper in becoming pregnant for the first time in your forties. Rocio hugged her again and said how delighted she was with the news.

"We didn't want to tell you before you came home," said her dad. "We didn't know how you would feel about the addition to the family and we wanted to be sure Sandra was well before you found out. So far all the signs are good. *El niño* will arrive in October *si Dios quiere.*" As they went to collect her case, Rocio felt a wave of homesickness or *morriña*, as her Grandmother would say. How would she cope if she was in England and her baby brother was here, growing up without her? It didn't bear thinking about. If only Galicia could find jobs for its graduates!

There were more surprises that evening. Having finished their meal (a bit late for Rocio who was used to dinner at 8:00 pm, not the Spanish 10:00 pm). her dad picked up a bunch of keys and said, "Rocio, come and *paseo* (walk) with me." She loved the way Galicians of all ages walked in the evening, escaping into the cooler evening air and sometimes having a drink but usually just greeting friends and passing the time of day, or more accurately, passing the time of night. As they walked, her dad jingled the keys in his pocket. They were obviously significant, and she wondered what other secret he had kept as they walked into the commercial district past the *Indianos* houses and the posh new boutique hotels and tapas bars. When they came to a white, freshly painted *local*, her dad stopped and took the keys from his pocket, unlocking the outer door.

"Step inside, love," he sang in English, copying the old Cilla Black song and making Rocio laugh at her father's fascination for sounds from the 60s. Inside, she was transported to a vision of Caranaby Street, a red post box was on one side (labelled "homework" above the slot), a park bench was situated on some Astroturf artificial grass, and street signs in English adorned the walls—very British!

"I love this place!" exclaimed Rocio. "But what on earth happens here? Whose are the keys?" It felt like stepping back to the UK seeing the various artefacts and posters for Billy Smart's Circus and holidays in Bridlington.

Her father looked at her for rather a long time before answering. "That depends on you, cariña. The keys are Sandra's. She has leased the *local* and was on the point of opening her own language school when she discovered your brother was on the way. She already has so many students signed up that the project is viable, but we don't think she will be able to teach after the first month of term, maybe less, if *el niño* arrives early like you did."

"Goodness gracious," she thought in her best English accent. She could hardly believe such a cool venue existed, let alone in her own *pueblo*, not the town most noted in the province for being hip or go ahead. And why did it depend on her? Did her father need her advice?

"Sandra thinks, with forty youngsters signed up and thirty adults ready to start, that she can afford to employ a teacher and still make a profit. She will get maternity allowance from her existing job and all she will need is to find a teacher, which is where you come in. Admittedly, you wouldn't be a *nativa* and you still have a whisper of Disney in your accent, but Sandra thinks you would be perfect for a full-time job and also would be able to teach Spanish and Gallego to the foreigners who are moving here or are wanting to have enough Spanish to apply for citizenship before the Brexit-exit starts. But, maybe your job in England is more important for your career."

"Not in the slightest, Dad! I would love nothing more than to come home, especially if I have a wee brother to get to play with. Do you think I could earn my keep? I am not a teacher, you know."

"Sandra already has all the classes worked out. You only need to deliver the materials, and once the baby is safely here she will help with those who need exam prep. She got me through my exams, remember, and it was you who helped me with all my homework." Rocio could hardly believe this opportunity—to be at home, working full time and close to not only her grandparents, but also with a new brother to get to know. Good things happen in threes, the Galicians say, and Rocio wondered what else could happen this holiday to make her joy complete.

After a tour of the two classrooms and coffee area, all very British, including English tea bags and a tin of digestive biscuits, her dad locked up and they resumed their *paseo* towards home. The night air was balmy, and as they walked through the square, they agreed to stop in Pedro's bar for a *cerveza* (beer). No sooner had they found a table than a voice called out to them, "¡Rocina!" Rocio hadn't been called that in years, but she knew the voice, it could only be Pepe, the son of the bar owner. He came across to wipe their table and take their orders. She was stunned to see the change in this guy, who had lost his student gawkiness and acne and was now a picture of glowing manhood. Her work colleagues would be surprised to see a Spanish man who was taller than they were and was neither bandy nor had any trace of a *barriga*, or beer belly. This bloke was gorgeous. How had that happened? He was asking about her: What had she been doing abroad, for how long was she home, and would she come out to the blues festival with him at the weekend? His dad apparently had free tickets for bar staff.

"I am not actually bar staff," he joked. "Dad doesn't pay me, but at least I have *enchufe* and get the perks!" Enchufe are the connections by which all Spanish culture gets things done in a form of communal back-scratching, not illegal usually and often an extremely helpful way around bureaucracy. They agreed to meet for the concert next evening, and he continued serving the punters, although how he could hear orders when they all talked loudly at the same time amazed Rocio, who was now more accustomed to quieter British pubs.

Her father was amused and clearly happy that these two had met again, Pedro was his friend and he could fill her in on the missing years when Pepe had travelled the world teaching surfing and had now come home to teach locally. The fact that he had won the Golden Board award in San Sebastian would be a draw as he built up clientele for his school. She realised that explained the perfectly toned body and the suntan. How funny that he might be coming home too.

When they arrived home, Sandra was resting, with her puffy ankles raised on a footstool. She looked anxiously at Guillermo to gauge how Rocio had reacted, but she needn't have worried.

"She loves the idea and really likes the décor of her new workplace. You have yourself a new teacher in time for the new school year." Guillermo was clearly relieved that his wife would not be overstretched. He initially had been very worried when he heard his wife described as a senile primigravida. The memories of his first wife's experience of presenile dementia had him momentarily panicked until Sandra reassured him it was just a medical term for an older mother and that she wasn't likely to go senile on him, although seeing how tired she was already, he thought she might fall asleep during the night feeds. She hugged Rocio as she went up to bed.

"Thank you so much for agreeing to come and fill the breach," Sandra said. "I was really hoping you would, but it might get very boring for you being here with so many of your friends still working abroad." Sandra caught Guillermo's eye as she spoke and he joked in English that Rocio might even "fill the beach" if she got involved with the new hot surfer. He would explain later.

After a week of holiday fun, visiting relations, and looking at prams with Sandra, Rocio returned to her job, just to give notice and pack up her flat, sell big things on eBay and pack small things in her three suitcases. Her boss looked really relieved that she was going. He admitted that things were flatlining for the company and a downturn was expected. Instead of a month's notice he was willing to pay her up front the next month's salary and she could leave as soon as she liked, with a glowing reference of her work and her impeccable English.

The next flight back to Santiago felt completely different from the previous one. She could not wait to touch down on the ground. She was eager to be truly home and no longer exiled by the economy. She recounted in her mind all the good things about Galicia. The list was endless today, with the greenery, scenery, beaches and peaches, caves and waves, towers and flowers. Already she was amassing lists in her mind to teach English in a way that was not based on grammar as she had been taught but to inspire her students with the sounds of useful words and help the process of remembering the right word in the right context.

When she came through the sliding doors this time there was no sign of her dad, but, instead, there stood Pepe. He took time to give her two kisses before he said she wasn't to worry but that her dad was with her stepmum in the hospital so he had been sent to collect her and bring her three cases in his camper van. This was such a cool vehicle. She loved the original Volkswagen colours and was glad he hadn't painted it with psychedelic decal panels. Apparently, he had lived aboard during his European travels. She was a tiny bit envious of the carefree lifestyle he had enjoyed while she was sitting behind a computer translating boring announcements. When she told him this he laughed and said there was still time to travel.

Pepe reassured her that Sandra was only admitted for observation due to high blood pressure and that Guillermo would be home later that evening. Meanwhile, could he invite her to lunch at the new beachside bar everyone was raving about? They stopped there to have a break on the long drive home, and soon they were settled on the beach at a log table made from the local eucalyptus planks. Galicia was becoming a real tourist magnet with superb on-the-beach cuisine. They finished their lunch and Rocio insisted on paying, to offset the cost of the fuel for his van.

"But I invited you, Rociña. It is our tradition—you can't pay, *profe*."

"What did you call me?"

"Rociña, I have always thought of you as Rociña wherever I have been in this world!"

"No not that, the other word. I could have sworn you called me *profe*" This was the informal word for a teacher, not offensive, really more affectionate. "I am not your teacher, Pepe."

"I was coming round to that, Rociña," he answered, smiling. "I need to get my intermediate English exam before next Summer. If I do, the council will fund me to teach English and water sports as a package. That would be real job security for my new business. When I asked your father's advice he assured me the best way to win a girl's heart was to sit and listen to her in class and then pass your exams. It worked for him! Sandra has me on your books!"

Slowly, she realised what he was saying. He had obviously been carrying a candle for her all the time he had been out of her circle. She smiled to think the old flame was still warm. This was her third welcome home gift. A new job, a new man, and in a couple of weeks maybe a new brother. As she thought of how good this felt, she felt her mobile vibrate in her pocket. Pepe gestured that she should go ahead and answer. It was her father's mobile number.

"¿Rocio? ¿*Gran hermana*?" a big sister already? My goodness, her dad's voice sounded excited. He reassured her by explaining that all was well with Sandra and that little Alejandro, his mother's namesake, was doing well. They were just waiting for the paperwork and they could be home later in the afternoon, waiting for her, waiting for Rocio's return.

~

Ribeira Sacra riverside village camino at Christmas.
Photo S Bush.

This Richly Crafted Paradise

by Liza Grantham
(Second place poetry)

As the chilly throes of winter finally ebb away
Its glistening, glassy world yields to a softer, gentler season,
Where Nature's silent seamstress tiptoes through the land,
Embroidering a vernal transformation.

Streams of silken strands are threaded through blankets of
emerald pasture;
Each random rendezvous twists them into silver skeins
As they dance through every Midas moment
Towards a distant destiny on shimmering shores.

In shaded woodlands where the mighty oak and chestnut are
canopied anew
A secret sylvan tapestry unfurls, as sunlight glances through
the glades
To cast its spell upon the strewn vestments of a colder,
darker time,
Gilding the patchworked hues of brown.

Legions of lofty eucalyptus stand triumphant on the hillsides,
Robed in regal verdigris and humbled only by the horizon,
Where a diadem of pine
Pierces the pinks and blues and mauves of the marbled sky.

The fabric of this verdant age is woven through the valleys:
A filigree of dew-kissed webs reaches out to thaw the heart of
twisted bramble,
And the gorse in golden glory parades its perfect pageant
Through this richly crafted paradise.

~

Galicia: The Switzerland of Spain. Annette M. B. Meakin

by Robin Hillard
(Third place non fiction)

Annette Meakin was an English freelance journalist and travel writer. She landed in Coruna in 1908, spent three months in Santiago, and travelled around the region, staying in Noya, Pontevedra, Orense, and Lugo. Modern travellers will enjoy comparing her journey with their experience in the twenty-first century.

This is not a book to be read from beginning to the final page, but rather treated as a library, with each chapter a volume in itself. After skimming the chapter headings, I started with Chapter 13, when Meakin arrives in Coruna. The city has changed since 1908, and her vivid description of the "narrow streets with toddling children, long legged pigs and poultry which swarmed in every direction" would be as foreign to today's residents as it is to an overseas visitor. One modern traveller, the blogger Kirtsy Hooper, decided to follow Meakin's journeys around the city and found "the principal sights (The Torre de Hercules or, the Tomb of Sir John Moore, for example) are still in existence, although their surroundings have changed hugely during the last century."

Hooper did most of her exploring on foot, and she wonders why Edwardian travellers drove to major sights instead of walking around the city. Considering the problem we have with the leavings of leashed dogs, I can imagine the condition of streets that were shared with pigs, hens, and teams of oxen in 1908. I would have joined Meakin in her carriage.

I wanted to know more about the pigs Meakin described. I went to Google and learned they were Porco Celta, a breed that was nearly lost when it was displaced by the faster-growing, imported pigs the writer preferred to the local animals. Modern readers will be pleased to know that the local breed is being revived, and though you'll no longer meet pigs on a city street, thanks to YouTube, you can watch some very happy piggiess snuffling around grassy fields and raising their babies in commodious, straw-filled pens.

Hooper would not have wanted to experience the earlier traveller's arrival in Coruna harbour. Meakin says "furious waves, working like yeast, break against the half-hidden rocks, and, rising to a stupendous height, swoop down upon them with thundering noise." She must have been alarmed when the sailors told her they "knew no more than I did about the coast, as neither they nor any of their line of steamers had ever entered that harbour before." She picked up the term "Costadel Morte" from the sailors, but it was probably her popular book that introduced the name to English readers.

It was a two-night voyage from Southampton to Coruna, and once safely on dry land, Meakin enjoyed exploring the country. In 1908 travelling between Betanzos and Ferrol took five hours by omnibus, and since there was no railway between Santiago and Noia, she had to spend another five hours in a coach to make that journey. After reading about her various excursions, the modern traveller, used to fast cars and planes, would question the writer's belief that, with some new railway lines and recently opened roads, the country was becoming more accessible. What she would think of the blogger Ed Ward, who tells us he can "leave my flat in Islington for the airport (with my one item of luggage) and be in *La Coruna* in *Galicia* with time to spare in four hours"? Would she miss the excitement of her more-complicated journeys?

One thing that has not improved in a hundred years is the behaviour of bureaucrats at a national border. Nowadays we are harassed in the name of security, but in 1908 officials were zealous in their search for contraband goods. Meakin was unlucky enough to arrive on a Saturday, when the customs house was closed, and she and her companion were ordered to leave their luggage on the quay. "May we not at least take a valise to the hotel with our night apparel?" she begged. No. Eventually, "finding at last that we were quite determined not to budge without the valise, they reluctantly handed it into our cab, and we drove off to an hotel."

Travelling between cities was hard enough, but Meakin was particularly interested in old monasteries that were not accessible by either road or rail. She describes the problems she had organising one such journey, a visit to the ruined monastery of Osera. "On my arrival at Orense I made many inquiries among my friends there as to the possibility of paying a visit to the ruins of Osera. One and all shook their heads. 'It is very difficult of access,' they said."

She eventually found an elderly priest "who told me that it was too rough an expedition for ladies, and that he himself had only been there once, and that was in his younger days." In spite of this discouragement, she continued her enquiries and eventually found a shopkeeper who gave her a letter to his lawyer brother, who lived in Osera. So equipped, she set out at 5.15 in the morning and drove seventeen miles in an open carriage, to a village at the end of the road. There she hired "a sturdy pony" that "picked its way between stones and boulders for a good two hours." When she reached Osera, she presented her letter of introduction to the shopkeeper's brother, who entertained her with hot chocolate and guided her around the ruins of the monastery.

She found the monastery well worth the difficult journey, and she bemoans the neglect of historical treasures. "It is sad, indeed, that Spain has not yet seen fit to make Osera a national monument, and that architecture, sculpture, and wood-carving of such high excellence should be left to rot and perish like things of no value." I wish she could visit the now-restored Monastery of Oseira, {https://en.wikipedia.org/wiki/Monastery_of_Santa_Mar%C3%ADa_de_Oseira} with its thirteen resident monks, tours, and accommodation for modern pilgrims.

Another difference between Meakin's experience in the beginning of the twentieth century and that of a traveller a hundred years later is illustrated by her visit to the ruined monastery of San Esteban de Rivas de Sil {https://es.wikipedia.org/wiki/Monasterio_de_San_Esteban_(Ribas_de_Sil)}. There is no accommodation, so she plans to take the railway to a little station in the valley, and, "after finding some cottager who could give me a night's shelter on my return, proceed to climb up to the ruins." When she arrived, there was only one cottage near the station, but, yes, she was given a bed. Can you imagine fronting up to an isolated farmhouse today and asking for a bed?

Not only did Meakin arrange to stay the night with strangers, but she also left her (unnamed) companion to be entertained by the cottager and, with two of the villagers as guides, scrambled down goat paths, crossed the river on a primitive raft, and climbed a steep slope to the monastery.

If you visit San Esteban de Rivas de Sil today, you won't have to knock on a cottage door to beg a bed, nor will you find a neglected ruin, because the monastery has been restored under a program established in 1928 by Alfonso XIII, to preserve historic buildings by converting them to luxury hotels. If Meakin could read the visitors' reviews of the Parador hotels in the old monastery of San Esteban de Rivas de Sil, and The Royal Hospital in Santiago, she would be thrilled to learn how many travellers share her love of the magnificent old buildings and appreciate the history held in their ancient walls.

The Royal Hospital of Santiago was built by Ferdinand and Isabella in 1492 to provide shelter for pilgrims and accommodation and nursing for the sick. In 1908, when Meakin was in Santiago, the building was serving as a hospital, but reading her description, you might, at first, believe this hospital to be as empty as the ruined monasteries. Only after a couple of thousand words exploring the building does she talk about the medical work of the hospital. Then she praises the care patients receive from the devoted nuns and surgeons "whose successful operations have earned them a good deal of fame." But she feels the wonderful old building is not really suitable for modern medicine, and I am sure she would approve of both the conversion of the Royal Hospital into a magnificent hotel and Galicia's modern health system.

Meakin's occasional mention of a companion and her use of the pronoun "we" left me wondering who shared her journey. In her account of their arrival in Coruna, she writes, "We were the only English on the boat," and later, while sightseeing, "We were glad of the hot sunshine," but on some of her more hazardous forays the pronoun changes to "I."

In an effort to satisfy my curiosity I went to Google again and learned that Annette Meakin and her mother were the first women to travel on the newly opened Siberian railway in 1900. Maybe Meakin's mother was with her to Galicia and used her extra years as an excuse to avoid the more energetic excursions.

Meakin spends three months in Santiago with this unnamed companion, and her chapters on the cathedral would serve as a useful guide for any modern traveller. Writing in 1908, she says, "the days of pilgrimages to the sepulchre of St. James are practically over." In 2018, with the popularity of the Camino de Santiago, the multinational crowd of modern pilgrims matches her description of a medieval pilgrimage, when Christians "flocked to Galicia from all parts of the known world".

Her interest in monasteries and pilgrimages is explained by her belief that "if the traveller really wishes to understand and appreciate Galicia or any other part of Spain, it is imperative that, side by side with the objects of interest that present themselves to his view, he should become acquainted with the story of Spain's glorious past. All who have studied Galicia are unanimous in their opinion that she contains more relics of that past and more trophies of antiquity than any other part of the Peninsula." And, true to this belief, she includes extensive quotes, ranging from Roman historians to contemporary authorities. She seems to have been on chattering terms with most of the experts in her field and equally at home with writers of antiquity. These earlier chapters should be saved for a lazy, rainy weekend, when they can be enjoyed with a cup of hot chocolate.

Occasionally, the author weaves her own experience into the material of her research. When she is describing the Cathedral of Santiago, she quotes an article written in 1889, describing how the chain of the Botafumeiro (the giant censer) broke and the censer, filled with burning charcoal, swung through the cathedral door and smashed on the ground. She adds that "the story appears to have been handed down from generation to generation among the townspeople of Santiago," as she heard it again from a local shopkeeper. That Botafumeiro was restored in 2006, and given the crowds of pilgrims backpacking along the Camino, the practical need for sweet-smelling incense might still be relevant.

Meakin is not an objective historian. She has great sympathy with the Middle Ages and rushes to the defence of the Visigoths, who she considers "the most cultured of all the barbarians of the north." After reading Meakin's account of the Visigoth kingdom, you might want to follow her to the only Visigoth church in Galicia, Santa Comba de Bande, in Orense {https://www.turismo-prerromanico.com/en/monumento/santa-comba-de-bande-20130420182340/}. She says it is much discussed by experts who read each other's accounts, but few have gone there. (The church now has its own website, and if you arrange a visit, the spirit of Meakin will bless you for taking the trouble.) I wonder if the inclusion of so much historical information in what was intended as a popular travel book was pushing a cause dear to the writer's scholarly heart, the proper care of Spanish medieval manuscripts, and the care and preservation of art and architectural treasures.

Together with her concern for historical buildings, art, and manuscripts, Meakin is anxious for the preservation of the Galician culture. Readers who have followed the arguments about Galicia's Celtic heritage will be fascinated by her account of the region's history that includes a description of the original Celtic tribes. They will also be interested in a conversation she had in Dublin. "An Irish maid who was assisting me to prepare for my departure, on hearing that Spain was the destination of my journey, remarked, 'That is the country my people came from. All the Irish came from Spain a long time ago.' 'Are you quite sure?' I asked. 'Yes,' she replied, 'quite sure. Everybody in Ireland knows that; even the poor people know it.'" She also refers to twentieth-century Gallegan peasants' weddings and the importance of local poetry events.

Meakin also champions the preservation of the Galician language, which, she says, was the language of "all Spain's greatest poets of the Middle Ages." She mourns its decline and rejoices in a possible revival with the emergence of Galician writers, especially the poet Rosalia de Castro. "Clear and distinct her poetic personality stands out from amongst all the rest; she has given the impulse, and others are already following in the path her genius has so clearly indicated, and a literary movement has been set on foot which may possibly terminate in a third Golden Age for Galicia."

Meakin is not totally uncritical of local beliefs. She visited the convent of Santa Clara, hoping to see a famous collection of relics. The nuns, a cloistered order, would not let her see the actual relics but gave her a booklet that included a list of the convent's treasures. This included drops of milk from both the virgin and St Catherine (drawn from the saint's breast by the knife of the executioner) and a collection of saints' skulls and bones. She "could not help feeling it was a good thing they were not on display."

Perhaps the nuns did believe in the authenticity of their relics, but those of us who grew up with television, to say nothing of the Internet and social media, find it hard to imagine how isolated some villages could be a hundred years ago. A conversation that could not happen today occurred when Meakin was visiting a little church on her way to Padron and talked to the priest's little maid.

"Why have you come so far to see such a poor little church as ours? And where have you come from?"

"I have come from England," I replied.

"Have they any religion in England?" she asked.

"Oh yes," I answered. "We have both religion and churches."

"But do they worship God there—and confess?"

"Yes."

"Then it must be in France where they have no religion!" she cried.

"Why do you think that?" I asked.

"Because they have turned all their monks and nuns out of the country, and now they have no church and no religion."

In 1908 she describes Galicia as "the least known and the least written about of all the little kingdoms that go to the making of Spain" and believes it was "the province that suffered most from the political unification of Spain," because it was "Governed at a distance and by strangers." I wonder what she would think of Galicia today. In 2018, thanks to the institution of autonomous regions, Galicia, like Catalona and the Basque Country, has its own regional government and Gallego is recognised as one of the region's two official languages. There is a thriving tourist industry, and pilgrims from all over the world flock to the Camino de Santiago.

Authors note:

If you are interested in comparing Galicia today with the country Meakin knew, you might enjoy these sites:

Kirtsy Hooper, Mapblogging. Streetscap Caruna). Hooper followed Meakin through Caruna.

https://www.youtube.com/watch?v=FYNhM_M6DWg. That's where I found the happy Galician pigs.

http://www.spanish-living.com/galicia/wild-galicia. Ed Ward makes the journey from Islington to Coruna in four hours.

~

Galicia–Land of Family and History

The Man of the Grapes

by Vanesa De La Puente Blanco
(First place non fiction)

Perfecto Blanco Robleda. This is the name of one of the most important people in my life; my grandpa. He died in 2010, eight years ago, but for me, he is still alive, because I remember him almost every day. He lives in my mind and in my heart. I can even feel his hands, old but strong, caressing my face when sleeping. I loved him. I love him. I will always love him.

My grandpa's story is very special for me, because he had to live lots of different moments in his life. He died in love with his life and with his motherland: Galicia.

He was born in a very small village called Alais in the heart of Galicia, a beautiful but still unknown place in Ourense, near the Sil River. This land is currently known as "A Ribeira Sacra". He grew up happily working in those marvelous lands, taking care about his family's lands and vineyards. He lived with his grandfather because of the death of his parents, but I know he had a lot of love in his childhood.

Things went worse when Spanish Civil War started, so he had to go to fight. He was good looking and young. He had already met the woman who was my grandmother and they were in love, but that is the way war works. He didn't even know what had happened for him to have to kill his "neighbors". At that moment, people who were friends became enemy forces. That's horrible!

It seems difficult to understand why people fight in those cases when they don't have any information about the reasons of the war. They lived without TV. Many people didn't have a radio or a newspaper to read in those small villages, so they found themselves with their men having to go to a war that they couldn't understand. Nobody can understand the war. No war is necessary, never. Although we don't like it, this is the way

69

our society unfortunately works, and the war was the reason he left his motherland to go to Madrid and Andalucía. My grandpa was one of those lucky men who went back home. He miraculously avoided death and he went back home.

He got married with María, my grandmother, and they built a family in the deepest Galicia, in his lovely Alais, in the same house where he was born.

In the sixties they decided to leave home and started a new life in Vitoria because of the economic situation. They worked in this marvelous city until their retirement, but my grandpa's real love was his Galicia, so they decided to return to Alais, leaving their descendants in Vitoria.

Why did they return to their origin? Because he never forgot the smell of Alais' sunrise, the colour of the grape leaves, nor the sound of the nature that you only can hear there. A Ribeira Sacra is the only place I know in the world where you can hear the sound of the silence. What a lexical contradiction! Go and discover it by yourself.

My lovely grandpa started to work in his lands again. Some of them were completely dead, but his hard work got the result he was looking for: great and healthy vineyards, where he collected delicious grapes to produce wine. My grandmother worked at home, and she took care of their animals: pigs, cows, rabbits . . .

Mencía is the name of the best-known grape in A Ribeira Sacra. My grandpa loved staying in the vineyards, taking care of the leaves and the grapes, deciding which leaf to pull out in order to let the sun caress the grapes. Every morning he walked to every one of their vineyard's corners, looking at the land and at the sky, praying and asking God not to let the storms hurt his beautiful leaves, his sweaty grapes, in fact, his heart. All his life he dreamed of having the best vineyards and cultivating the best wines. I actually know they were not the best ones in the world, but I´m sure they became that in his dreams.

In the afternoons, he walked holding my grandmother's hand, showing her his work. She always admired him. He always admired her. They respected and loved each other. They were very tender and the best couple I have ever known.

When staying in A Ribeira Sacra you can live an incredible natural experience. High and strong trees, mountains that hide small villages, Romanic art in churches and monasteries, roads with a million curves, and, of course, the principal characters of the place, the rivers: Cabe, Sil, and Miño.

There are many lookouts where you can see the whole valley—magic places because of the views. In the north side of the rivers, trees; in the south, vineyards with infinite gradients. Heroic wine producing, as it is nowadays known, is what people over the years have been doing in order to produce wine in those lands. Wine producers in A Ribeira Sacra are heroes.

In some cases, grape harvesting is done from the river with small boats, because it is impossible to get up the side of the hills. There are some vineyards with rails to help the work. My grandpa loaded up big baskets full of grapes over and over again until everything was collected. After the work, people celebrated the good vintage by all having a nice meal together, and nowadays wine producers of course celebrate the harvest, of course they do. That's a special party in these marvelous lands.

Perfecto Blanco Robleda died in 2010 when he was ninety years old. I remember that moment. because it has been the biggest loss in my life. He kissed my hand and my belly before dying when I was pregnant with my first daughter, Izaro. She was born fifteen days after that sad moment for me. I wanted him to know her and I still sometimes cry because it didn't happen. He loved babies, he loved me, and I'm sure he would have loved Izaro with all his big but weak heart. In a way, I feel that a part of him lives in Izaro.

My grandmother told Izaro and my small child, Julen, a lot of stories about their youth. She loved her life and she always talked about my grandpa with love. She died one month ago. I miss her.

Last year I stayed for a week in my grandparent's house in Galicia with my family. We visited some touristic places in A Ribeira Sacra. For my children and my husband that is a place to go on holiday. For me, it is the place where I feel nearest my grandpa. That time my grandmother was still alive so I don´t know how I will feel the next time I visit their empty house.

People who visit Galicia usually only visit the coastline, forgetting the heart of the land. What a pity! Galicia is like a five-star hotel, where you can find everything you need and everything you want: mountains, beaches, good food, great wines . . .

I love Galicia because it means loving my grandparents. For their unconditional love, for their hugs, for their words, and for teaching me to close my eyes and feel the freedom of the nature. Galicia was their cot and I am sure their souls dance to the rhythm of the wind there.

I love you, Grandpa. I love you, Grandma.

~

Mencía Grapes growing in the Ribeira Sacra region.
Photo S Bush.

The Legend of Rosalia de Castro
by Barbara Mitchell

Rosalia,
Woman
Feminist
Heroine
Icon
Poetess

Rosalia,
How you struggled.
How you suffered.
How you conquered!

Rosalia,
How you are remembered.
How you are honoured.
How your words are loved.

Rosalia,
The spirit of this wondrous place called Galicia.

~

A Tale of a Xaicia

by Noellia Roca Jones
(Second place fiction)

Galicia is a beautiful place, covered in luscious vegetation and home to many different animals. It also has numerous tales and legends full of mystery. When I was a child I loved to listen to the old tales of Galicia, the "Santa Compaña", the witches (*meigas*), and so on, but the tales that truly fascinated me were the ones about the "*xacios*". I used to search in books for stories about them and ask elderly people what they knew about them, and the more I heard the more I believed in them. I have always loved swimming and I always said maybe in another life I had been a xacia.

A xacia, one could say, had an unusual appearance, similar to the mermaids of northern fairy tales. It was considered a mythological being, with a body that was half fish and half human. It lived in the deepest pools in the mighty Galician rivers, hidden from human eyes.

I have heard so many stories of xacios, and they were all very similar. Fishermen who claimed to have seen them or their family members who accompanied them on their fishing jaunts had spotted them.

My curiosity was aroused, so one summer morning during my school holidays, I decided to visit one of my uncles. He was one of my dad's brothers, with whom I had had little contact as he lived alone, far from the city, in a small house near the river Miño. When I got to his house, he received me kindly, although he was a little confused as to why I was visiting him. He made himself an iced coffee and cocoa for me, and we sat on the settee next to the huge windows that looked out onto the river. The truth be told, the house was cosy and the views spectacular. It was such a shame that he did not care to have visitors, I would have loved to spend some afternoons there, or even nights when we could gaze at the star-filled sky and tell ghost stories.

When we were settled on the settee, I explained why I was visiting him. I told him all the stories I had heard from the many fishermen I had spoken to and I asked him if he knew any stories, if he had ever seen a xacia. As I was explaining my interest in these creatures to him, the expression on his face changed, becoming hardened. He got really angry, jumping up from the settee and telling me never to ask him about that again. Then he stormed out of the door. I had no idea what was going on. I just stood there, stunned, with tears in my eyes, not knowing what to do. I knew I had done nothing wrong, so I couldn't understand why he had reacted like that, nor why he had shouted at me. Still not knowing what to do, I called my mum in floods of tears and asked if she could come and fetch me. When she came, I told her all about it. She told me to forget it and not to bother speaking to him again.

I tossed and turned that night, trying to figure out what I had said that could have upset him so much, I still didn't understand what was wrong. After going over it all in my head, I finally dropped to sleep.

Several days later, I had put it all out of my mind. I had decided I would not speak to him again about the matter. I wasn't aware of any reason for his reaction, but it was just better not to bring it up again.

A couple of weeks later, he contacted me. He phoned me one afternoon, asking me to visit him as soon as I could and apologising for his behaviour. I wasn't very sure it was the right thing to do, but I agreed to go back to his house. I didn't tell my parents where I was really going but pretended I was going to see Diana, my best friend. I caught the bus that took me to the village and from there I walked to his house. I was going over everything in my head, wondering why he now wanted to see me.

I finally arrived at his house. He greeted me as warmly as on the previous occasion, but in his face I could see traces of guilt and shame for the way he had treated me before. He asked me to sit down on the big, cosy settee, and while I was getting comfortable, he left the room. He came back shortly, carrying a dusty old album. I was more bemused than ever.

He sat beside me and started talking. First, he asked me what I knew or had heard about the xacios. I told him all that I had read about them and what I had been told by other people. He smiled and said much of it was true. I was more and more confused by the turn things were taking. Suddenly, his face became serious, or maybe to be more concise, concerned. He said I must never reveal to anyone what he was about to tell me. Obviously, I promised to keep the secret. I knew something was wrong. Perhaps it was the reason for his unfriendly manner to others and his antisocial behaviour. I wanted to prove he could trust me, that even though I was still a child I could be relied on not to tell anyone what he was going to tell me. Once he was reassured on this matter, he began his story:

"It all happened one summer morning, exactly ten years ago to the day. I was getting ready to go fishing, as I often did, unaware that my life was going to be changed forever. I got my nets and rods ready and started the little outboard motor on my fishing boat. As soon as I reached my destination, I turned off the engine, set up my rods and nets, and leaned back to enjoy the beautiful summer day. It was getting close to midday, and I was getting ready to leave after catching several fish when I felt a strong tug on my net. I tried to haul it in but whatever it was was too strong for me. In the end, I managed to pull it in but the net was torn. But that wasn't the strangest thing, even stranger were the scales the fish had left on the net and a strand of what looked like human hair. Even so, I didn't give it much thought beyond being annoyed at having torn my net. After dinner, I started wondering what kind of fish could have done that. Well, I thought I will go out in the morning to see if I can find it and I went to sleep.

"The following morning I repeated my routine, getting my tackle and boat ready and setting off. This time I intended to be on the lookout for the strange fish. What I never expected was that it would turn out not to be a fish but something much lovelier. By midmorning I had given up all hope of finding it and I was getting ready to leave, when I saw something that left me speechless. There was a woman in the water. I brought the boat closer to ask if I could help her and I saw something absolutely unbelievable. She smiled at me and refused my help. Then she dived into the water and I saw a huge blue, scaly tail. I was so stunned that I just stood there, unable to move for about a quarter of an hour, not knowing what to say, do or think.

"I finally went home, going over in my mind the sequence of events. I thought to myself: No way! I had heard many stories but had never believed them. They were fishermen's tales, unreal and imaginary. Now what? I couldn't tell anyone what I had seen. No one would believe me. They would call me crazy and they would laugh at me. I was unable to sleep a wink that night. I tossed and turned . . . until finally I knew what I had to do. I would take the boat out in search of whatever it was that I had seen. I circled with the boat, backwards and forwards, in the spot where I had seen her. Then I decided to turn the engine off and wait for her to appear again. And suddenly it happened. I saw her in the water. She was so beautiful, with big blue eyes and long brown hair. She smiled as she came closer. I was speechless. I didn't know what to say. Was I dreaming? Was she real?

"We started to speak. She told me her name was Meredith, which meant Lady of the Sea. "She explained how they, the xacios, had lived for many, many, years, hidden in the river. That the legends had some basis of truth because they did, indeed, exist. They had occasionally been spotted by humans, but not by as many as claimed to have seen them . . . but you know what it's like . . . one person sees one and suddenly everyone else has too.

"We met several times, always at night when no one else was out on the river, so no one would discover her. They were afraid of being caught by humans, of being examined, so they remained as hidden as possible.

"In time, we fell in love and that was the beginning of my worst nightmare. She told me that if she was baptised, the spell would be broken. So, I called a distant family member, whom I trusted and who was a priest. The baptism took place. Being half fish half human, they were able to live both in the water and on land. She had become disenchanted with life in the river, so we decided to live in my home."

As my uncle told his story, I was spellbound. Was it possible that they existed? Why had he never told anyone his story? Where was his partner really from? I was becoming more and more fascinated, but as he continued with his story his voice started to quiver. I couldn't help myself and blurted out: "Uncle, why did you never tell anyone about Meredith? What really happened?" To which he answered, "Sshhh, little one. Soon you will understand everything. Let me go on."

And so he carried on telling me his story: "At first, everything was wonderful. We were deeply in love and everyone who met Meredith thought she was sweet and delightful. She got on well with everyone. She was happy, or so I thought. As the years went by, I realised she missed the water and her old life. She missed her loved ones, and although she tried to hide it, deep down I was aware of this. One morning, I went out to do some shopping and when I came home, the house was ominously silent. I feared the worse and rushed into the bedroom, and there on the bed, on our marriage bed, there was a note that said:

"'To the love of my life: I am so sorry for leaving like this. I wanted to explain to you but I didn't know how. I know this is not the right way to do things and you don't deserve this. I miss my old life even though I am happy with you. Inside, something tells me that my life is in the water, with my own kind. I hope you will forgive me and not hate me too much. I will always love you.'

"I felt a stabbing pain in my heart. I didn't want to believe it was true. Why was this happening to me? Why hadn't she told me and we could have found a way together? My heart was breaking and I just wanted to die.

"For a week, I wouldn't go fishing and I shut myself away in my house, refusing to go out or to see anyone. When I had had enough of being indoors, I realised I didn't deserve that, I would go out fishing as I usually did. That day . . . I will never forget that terrible day. When I went to get my boat, I came across Meredith's body, dismembered, she had been killed in the vilest manner. I phoned the police, unable to believe what had happened. I couldn't stop crying, I kept vomiting, I was having panic attacks. The police came and questioned me endlessly. For a time, I was their one and only suspect. No one could explain what had happened, nor could I. How could they believe that I had committed that atrocity to the one person I loved most in the world? I was acquitted of all charges. There was no evidence to convict me, obviously, because I hadn't done it. But all the neighbours, all the people who had adored Meredith, thought I had. They thought I was guilty. So, I made the decision to lock myself away in my home, to never receive anyone, ever.

"Some time later, while I was searching for an answer to it all, I found out the truth. Meredith had told me that if she was baptised, the spell would be broken. But what she never told me was, that if she was baptised, if she became a Christian, the other xacios would turn against her and if ever she dared to return to the water, they would kill her."

When my uncle finished telling me his story, I didn't know what to say. Now I understood everything, his behaviour, why he didn't want to talk about it. I suppose he never told anyone the truth in order to protect the xacios and therefore carried the burden alone, stoically. My eyes were brimming with tears, and I couldn't say anything. How unfair is life, I thought. He turned to me and put the photo album in my hands. He said it contained all the photos they had ever taken together from the beginning to the end of their life together. He told me to treasure the album; that it was for my eyes only, not to show it to anyone else. At that moment, I felt I was the luckiest person on Earth. Not only had he told me his secret, he had also given me his most precious memories of Meredith. When he gave it to me, I hugged him so hard he could barely move. I assured him that his secret was safe with me. From then on, we became even closer. He slowly started to leave the house and mix with people again. I would suggest going for a walk, to go for a pizza . . . and in the end he started to live a normal life again. Though, the pain of Meredith's loss would remain in his heart forever.

~

Here Be Dragons

by J. P. Vincent

"I can see it; I can see it," chanted Ainoe, her chubby hand pointing to a dark hole in the mossy trunk. "Race you," she giggled.

"Wait for me." Her older sister followed her, also spying the hole. The clearing had been trampled. They weren't first.

"Pick me up; pick me up," Ainoe squealed excitedly. "I've got it." She shoved her hand in the hole and pulled out a box.

"Careful. It might be fragile." Ainoe tried to prize the lid off. She pulled, flicking and scraping her nails. Nothing. The gold tin box refused to open.

"Here, let me look." Ainoe passed the box and gently levered off the bent and twisted lid.

"What's in it?" She pulled on her sister's arm to get a better look. In the bottom, on a bed of tissue, lay small, marked eggs. "What does it say?"

"Here be Dragons."

"Is that the next clue?"

"Yep." The two girls carefully lifted out one of the eggs and placed it gently in the small basket, along with several other objects and their clues written in a fine, curly green ink script. The younger girl furrowed her brow, deep in thought.

"Come on, Iria. I know the answer. It's the church," Ainoe announced gleefully. For once she had found the answer all by herself. The dragons in question were on each corner of the small stone church that had stood in the village for two hundred years, a centre for a dwindling community. Over the years, many had left the village to find work or marry, or they were pushed out for their political leanings. Those who were now left were old or only returned to their family homes for the summer to escape the heat of the big cities. Iria and her younger sister, Ainoe, were just two of them.

* * * *

The dragons in reality were the griffin gargoyles that, when it rained, spouted water from the roof and away from the church, an impressive sight during a typical Galician inundation. The girls ran to the church.

"The door's open," puffed Ainoe. "Will our next clue be inside?" The girls stood on the granite step under the arched doorway. The cool air wafted past their bare legs and caused the hairs to stand on end. After the brightness of the July sun, the darkness inside created its own barrier. "I don't like this," Ainoe said. She took a step back and caught hold of Iria's T-shirt.

"It's OK," Iria answered. Her words sounded more confident than she felt. "I'm sure Tio Paco wouldn't hide the clue inside. It would be sacrilege. Let's go round the back." Round the back housed the village's dead in above-ground tombs. Iria and Ainoe's family tombs were there, containing the remains of ancestors long gone. Tio Paco spent many hours telling the girls and their cousins the stories of their ancestors. Each time the telling became more elaborate, with more bravery and heroism and always ending with Tio Paco sobbing into a large white hankie. The two girls rummaged in the bright plastic flowers laid each year to commemorate the dead. They scrabbled around under the bushes directly beneath one of the griffin gargoyles. Nothing. "Perhaps we have to look higher?"

"I see it. I see it!" Ainoe cried out. White and black feathers dangled in midair attached by a thin blue ribbon. Ainoe jumped and jumped, but she was too small to reach it. Iria tried, but the feathers were too high.

"Fetch a stick, Ainoe." The little girl ran, looking over the low wall that surrounded the church, along the path. Nothing.

"There's nothing."

"I'll go into the church. There's a broom in the vestry." Once a year their abuela, grandmother, Tio Paco's sister, and the remaining elderly ladies cleaned the church from top to bottom in readiness for the service on their saint's day and the village fiesta. Iria had helped her abuela this year and knew where the brooms were kept. The interior of the church was silent, dark, and smelled of polish. The cool air was still escaping from the darkness to greet the light and warmth as she ventured through the open door. Apart from the cleaning days, the annual service, and the misas for the dead, the church is always kept locked. There was nothing left to steal that had all gone during Franco's time, the time when Tio Paco cried the loudest for the loss of dead ancestors. She was a little apprehensive, the church always felt light and happy when it was full of ladies with their buckets, brooms, and singing of traditional songs, but today, there were no adults, no light or noise. There just were the coolness of the interior and darkness. Her eyes adjusted to the dimness and she could see the altar and the rows of crudely made benches.

"Hurry up, Iria," her sister called, her voice faint through the stone walls.

"OK," Iria answered. She rushed over the stone step up the aisle and into the vestry. The broom cupboard wasn't locked, but the handle was stiff. She twisted it with a force brought on by fear, and the door flew open and brooms clattered onto the stone floor. She grabbed one and dashed out, only to be blinded by the hot light of the sun. A pair of arms encircled her, and she looked up in terror, unable to see anything beyond a dark shape above her. She squealed. Her broom fell to the ground with a crack.

"What are you doing in the church?" A low voice asked. She was still blinded by the bright sunlight and didn't recognise the voice or the smell of tobacco that enveloped the arms around her.

"I'll scream," she cried in a high-pitched voice. "My Tio Paco will hear me." The stranger laughed.

"No, he won't. He's taken Abuela up to the campo to prepare supper for all you treasure hunters." This statement took her by surprise.

"Oh," she said. Her sight returned and the big dark shadow became clearer. He looked as old as Tio and Abuela, the same crinkly eyes from being too long in the sun, the same sticky out ears that everyone in the family suffered from, but she'd never seen him before.

"I'm your Tio Pepe."

"But you're dead. Tio Paco cries loudest when he tells your story." Pepe smiled down at her, unwrapping her from his embrace, and said sadly, "Unfortunately, my story isn't the one Paco tells."

"Oh. You were killed by Franco's spies."

"Not quite."

"Iria, have you got the broom?" Iria had forgotten Ainoe was waiting for her to knock down the feather.

"Yes, coming. How did you get into the church?" She asked her tio.

"One of the neighbours has a spare key."

"So, Tio Paco and Abuela don't know you're here then?"

"No, they don't. I wanted to surprise them, but first I wanted to look round the village and the church." He smiled. "Then I met you."

"Iria, come on. I'm getting hungry."

"We'd best get our next clue." Iria said and sShe took Pepe round the back.

"Who's that?" Ainoe whispered loudly.

"Tio Pepe."

"But he's dead and Tio Paco . . ."

"Yes, we've been through all that."

It was Ainoe's turn to say, "Oh." She took hold of Iria's hand, moved behind her, and stared up at the stranger.

"Hello, Ainoe. How are you?" Pepe asked.

"Fine." She turned to Iria. "What about the next clue? I want to see what's written on the feather." Pepe pulled the feather and it broke away from its thread and passed it to Ainoe. She read out loud.

"Now you've come this far and found dragons, it's time to fly. Use this feather to find its owner and there you'll reach your goal and collect your prize." The same green, curly script as on the other objects.

"What sort of feather is it?"

"It's a stork," Iria replied. "There's a stork's nest by the campo."

"Let's run. Are you coming, Tio Pepe?"

"Yes, but less of the running."

* * * *

At the campo they found some of their cousins and neighbours' families gathered around a long table laid out with food and drink. A BBQ pit was lit and ready for cooking, manned by Tio Paco, and the elderly villagers seated were waiting for everyone, including the last treasure hunters, to arrive.

Abuela was the first to spot them walking toward the feast. "A vision, *madre mia*, a holy vision," she cried.

The others turned to see what Abuela was on about.

"Yes, truly a vision," they chorused, stood up, and rushed over to the two girls and "the vision." They were swamped by the small crowd, all trying to hug, kiss, and touch "the vision." Tio Paco cried the loudest and Abuela wiped her tears away on her apron. All were asking questions: "Where have you been?" "What are you doing here?" "Do you have children?" and so forth.

Ainoe whispered to Iria, "Where's our prize?"

"Shush, not now."

"But we were promised a prize if we got all the clues and we did." She looked forlornly at their little basket of objects and back to the throng still kissing, hugging, crying, and asking questions.

"First, let's eat and then Pepe can tell us how he escaped the spies," Paco said, grinning down at the girls. "And Pepe can hand out the prizes to the treasure hunters."

"Who's for a rib?" said someone.

"Yes, please," The gathered throng chorused in reply. Minutes later, they were tucking into ribs, steaks, sausages, and delicious Galician bread and were drinking wine, but only grape juice for the children. Tio Paco cleared his throat. "Now, Pepe, your story." All eyes turned to Pepe, who, in turn, appeared a little shy at this sudden focus.

"Yes, Tio Pepe, did Franco's spies really beat you up, like Tio Paco tells us, before he cries?"

"Yes, they did," begins Pepe. "The soldiers from Madrid were taking all the food from the village to feed the people in the cities. If they'd taken part or even half, it probably would have been OK, but they didn't. Paco, Papa, and I were hiding food up in the mountains, in caves, in the dry mill races under the mills, anywhere we could find. A small group of soldiers found us as we were carrying the hams from that year's *metanza* (pig killing)." Tio Paco nodded sadly. "We had to eat as well! At the point of rifles, they took the hams. I held onto mine and ran. They chased me up the paths and caught me near the little shrine by the casa of the Vazquez family." The elderly nodded, remembering. "They took the ham, knocked me over, and hit me with their rifle butts. I was bleeding badly. Two teeth had gone and I thought they'd broken my arm." The children stared at him and checked for missing teeth. He laughed. "I've got new ones. Anyway, the soldiers decided to try their luck at the Vazquezes." They nodded. "And whilst they were occupied, I ran up the old sheep track into the mountains."

"But we heard shots and they showed us the ravine you'd fallen into," cried Tio Paco. "We never found your body. We searched for many months. We thought the bears or wolves had taken you. It was a lean time for all of us." He sighed.

"No, they didn't shoot me. I was too far away by then. The shots were ones of anger only—anger that they hadn't beaten me enough to keep me down and they'd probably found the wine." Abuela poured the enthralled audience another drink and Tio Pepe continued. "I ran, or more correctly, hobbled, for several days north up to the coast. I stole corn from the *horreos* (raised Galician grain stores), eggs from chickens and *grelos* (turnip tops) from the gardens, they're disgusting uncooked!" He laughed. "I arrived at night in Burela and scoured the bars for someone to take me across to France or England. One bartender took pity on me, fed me, and let me wash up. I was covered in dry blood; I was filthy and must have smelt really bad." Ainoe wrinkled her nose. "I went and hid by the fishing boats and waited. At first light the crews came down to their boats and I begged them to take me. I had no money, it was dangerous, and I didn't know who I could trust, but luck was on my side and the first crew said they would take me to Bordeaux." He took a large slug of wine from his glass.

"Then what happened?" Ainoe asked.

"Shush, Ainoe, let Tio Pepe tell it in his own time," Abuela interrupted the little girl. Tio Pepe ruffled Ainoe's hair and grinned.

"It was a long, hard journey, and eventually I made it to Venezuela, where I've lived ever since, No, I never married and I don't have children. I worked for the UN as a lawyer, trying to bring a little justice to this world. I've retired and I wanted to come home." Tio Paco brought out his hankie and howled uncontrollably. Abuela wiped the tears from her apron, and the children looked bewildered, surrounded as they were by another emotional outpouring.

"What about our prizes?" Ainoe whispered to Iria.

"Ah, glad you mentioned that. I have a bag that I left by the church with gifts for everyone." Tio Pepe announced.

"Oh goodie," cheered Ainoe. She clapped her hands and brought the emotional party back to the present day.

~

Church door. Photo by J. P. Vincent.

Where's My Ghost?

by Liza Grantham

Our house is really ancient,
And it's made of stone and wood.
It has a lot of quirky bits,
As every old house should.

The downstairs is a cattle pen,
With standing stones for stalls,
An earthen floor and cobwebbed beams
And mildew on the walls.

Upstairs the floor boards creak and groan,
The doors don't fit quite right.
The windows shake and rattle
And the wind blows through at night.

By moonlight bats swoop o'er the roof,
The village graveyard looms,
The owls screech from the nearby woods,
And mice dart through the rooms.

It might sound rather spooky,
But there's no need to be daunted—
Although it's stood two centuries,
Our house just isn't haunted!

No lonely spirit walks at night,
No hidden spectre's peeping,
No apparition brushes past,
Or watches while we're sleeping.

I'd really love to have a ghost
That creeps from room to room.
Or rattles doors and screams out loud,
Or howls and wails in gloom.

Perhaps our house *was* haunted once,
Perhaps our spook was banished,
Perhaps it learned to rest in peace,
But either way it's vanished!

I've searched each nook and cranny,
Ev'ry pillar, plank and post,
Each cubby-hole and corner,
So please tell me, where's my ghost?
~

An Intriguing Life
in Galicia

At Market In Antas

by Liza Grantham
(First place poetry)

At market in Antas it's drizzling again.
I'm under the bandstand, away from the rain.
I've just set my stall out in spite of the weather.
Already I'm reaching the end of my tether:

The wind's blowing fiercely, my stuff's on the floor!
As fast as I catch it, it's flying once more!
Thank goodness for Fruit Man who runs to my aid:
I'm soon relocated with nerves somewhat frayed.

I light up a ciggie, I'm instantly calmed,
But Fruit Man runs over; he looks most alarmed:
In here it's 'No Smoking', the sign's on the wall,
So I stub it out quickly and tend to my stall.

I look at Cold Meat Man who chain smokes all morning
As he doles out chorizo from under his awning.
I wonder what makes him exempt from the rule,
But I'm not going to argue; it's best to keep cool.

I notice Big Pants Girl has come with her child,
Who's bored in the pushchair, and growing quite riled
I take her a pony, she looks up and beams,
Mum gives me some knickers with lace down the seams.

I see that Cheap Shoe Girl's been shivering for hours
There aren't many people out due to the showers.
I feel pretty sure she's sold nothing all day,
At a quarter to one she starts clearing away.

I give up at half past, my takings are zero,
But Fruit Man comes over, thank God, what a hero!
He looks at the hedgehogs and tells me they're pretty.
Buys two for his daughters, I'm sure it's just pity!

95

At market in Antas I've stood here for hours:
I've suffered the wind and the cold and the showers;
I've taken twelve euros since I got here at ten,
But I'm pleased with my knickers, so I *will* come again!

~

Roof, Table, Door. Possible Turner Prize Winner?

by J. P. Vincent

The last time I visited the Tate Modern Gallery not only did I mistake the new air-conditioning system in the large hall for an exhibit but I couldn't believe that "Shed, Boat, Shed" was the Turner prize winner for that year. Basically, a bloke, or to quote The Tate's Web page, "artist Simon Starling dismantled a shed and turned it into a boat; loaded with the remains of the shed, the boat was paddled down the Rhine to a museum in Basel, dismantled and re-made into a shed. Both pilgrimages provide a kind of buttress against the pressures of modernity, mass production and global capitalism." In my humble opinion it was a perfectly good shed that had a useful function whilst it was a shed and remains useful whilst it is a shed or boat, for that matter. Seeing the photos of the boat, I think it was little more than a raft that a group of youngsters could knock up with their dads over a long weekend. Why it won any art prize is beyond me.

However, I have roof, table, door. I wonder if it'll win any prize? All stages of its life functional, useful, and pleasing to look at, which is enough for me.

"I am very fortunate", so says my sainted better half, John, for we live next door to a builder! He, the builder, renovates old properties as the client requests, with concrete beams, holey bricks, and tiled rooves. Nothing whatsoever wrong with that, and it's to our advantage because we renovate using old chestnut beams, boards, slates, or loso, and stone. Three years ago our neighbour, the builder, turned up in his lorry and dumped several loads of our favourite products, chestnut beams, chestnut and oak roof boards, large slates that took two of us to lift, and hefty granite rocks. John's eyes gleamed with joy. "All this could be ours," he cried with delight.

"OK," I replied not so enthusiastically. "He might need it or he could be going to reuse it all," I responded.

A few days later the builder returned in his lorry. The choice products had remained in a large heap in the middle of his mum's old huerta, now his building yard, and John couldn't contain his patience any longer and trotted down to see him and to enquire, in a casual fashion, of course, what was he going to do with all that rubbish. He returned, grinning from ear to ear. The builder was going to burn it or break it all up to create hardcore for his yard. Obviously, his mum wasn't going to get her huerta back in the near future. So, yes, it would help him out if we took what we wanted.

Out came Kylie, John's one-and-a-half-ton digger, and off we went to bring back our bargains. We brought back fifteen or so large chestnut beams, one of which was seven meters long and so heavy it tipped the digger over with John in it! A scary moment, I can tell you. Small roof spars, again chestnut, which are now holding up the ceiling under the balcony. Floor and roof boards that were nearly an inch thick, blackened with smoke from years of cooking fires. Slates, or loso, which were the old roof, covered with moss and lichens and so beautifully weathered that I couldn't stop stroking them.

Huge great things they were and took two of us to carry. Finally, large river boulders and granite rocks, some of them shaped and formed. In all a grand haul and at the time about to be repurposed, reused, or recycled, whichever is your preferred term. My favourite expression, which has stood the test of time and tight budgets, is "waste not, want not". Everything then had to be stored somewhere and you can't really hide seven-metre beams behind the sofa. John, with his trusty Kylie, and I stacked all the slate and stones near the front gate, the beams behind the house, and the boards under a tarpaulin at the top of the garden. And there they stayed until we commenced our various projects in the garden.

The weather here in Galicia during the winter is normally wet and sometimes it gets us down and we try to spend at least a month away in the dry and warm, but last Christmas we decided to brave the wet, cold, and dark of December and stay at home. Part of this decision was because we'd had several Christmases on our own and felt left out of the celebrations and we wanted to spend this time with our friends. We invited, and our invitations were accepted by, six of them. Oh dear. We didn't have a table big enough. Our existing table sat four comfortably and six at a squeeze but never eight. John said, "I'll make a table top to fit over the existing one."

"Good idea," I said, "and can I have it raised bit in the middle like a lazy Susan but not on a turntable?"

"OK," he cheerfully replied, and off he toddled up the garden to his stack of smoke-charred roof boards. A great deal of noise, a flurry of activity, and a fair bit of whistling went on for the rest of the day.

That evening he brought in his prize, a table top that would fit up to ten people. Roll on Christmas. The long, curved, charred boards he'd planed until most of the burnt was gone—not all; we wanted a bit of character. He'd waxed the surface until it shone and screwed the pieces together using a couple of spars on the reverse to create a beautiful top with slightly curved edges. And along the middle he'd used a piece of live edge timber to create a raised area for the hot food, no need for mats or tablecloth. It was far too beautiful to cover up. The raised piece had been sawn, originally by hand, with a two-man saw. The evenness of the saw marks were a joy to behold. I know this because, as a child, I used to sit and watch my granddad and uncle saw planks and they were proud of their neat, precise saw marks. I was probably a strange child.

Christmas was a roaring success. We had quizzes and crackers that we shouted "Bang" to when they were pulled, because there weren't any crackers in Spain and we weren't allowed to bring in the "bangs" due to new firearms regs. We're not sure if they were English, Spanish, or European regulations. Our challenge that day was to try and synchronise eight people to pull crackers and say "bang" at the same time. It was nigh on impossible, especially when one of our party couldn't wait and had opened hers already. The food was delicious, cooked in our kitchen. But everyone contributed something, and thanks to the new table top being wider and longer, with a raised bit in the middle, we all sat comfortably, ate well, and played games.

We've used our table top on more than one occasion, the latest being this year for our double-zero birthday bash, but it was only needed for the cutlery and glasses during lunch.

For our double-zero birthday bash eight people were staying in our little house. Every one of the beds was taken up, and even the sitting room floor slept three people. The oldies got the bedrooms and the youngsters pretended they were at boarding school, complete with midnight feasts, lots of giggling, and copious amounts of wine.

John and I slept in the shed. The shed in question had only been found last year under fifty-odd years of stones, brambles, and small trees. We honestly didn't know it was there until one of our workaways, Fernando, decided he was bored and wanted to clear this part of our garden. Two weeks later all four crumbling stone walls and a dirt floor were uncovered and mountains of rubbish duly had been sent to the tip, but the shed was minus a roof, windows, and a door. Ahead lay a summer of renovation and rebuilding of the two-foot-thick stone and mud walls with stones recently cleared from inside "the shed" and some cement. The exposed walls where the rain had washed most of the mud away had to be underpinned, the arch over the well door had to be rebuilt, and three of the walls had to be built up to a reasonable roof height. We had to create new window openings for good airflow and to keep the damp to a minimum and add a new roof using the beams from our stockroom supplied by next doors building rubbish. We did, however, have to buy new planks and insulated roof panels.

John added a roof light, using toughened glass bought from our favourite, I think only, charity warehouse in Lugo. A new workspace was created. We decided it was to be a project room and not to be filled up with tools, equipment, and stuff. This lasted about two days and up to a week before our party housed the mixer, timber, scaffold frame, and so forth. Once the shed was cleared, we laid a mattress on the benches, built especially for the project room, before it was filled with stuff. We had a cosy! dry! quiet! space to sleep in whilst our guests claimed the bedrooms and floorspace of our little stone Galician house.

During the two weeks around the party and with a full house, we realised how cosy our "shed" was. All of the local cats, including ours, would wander in, take over, sleep on any flat surface, and unfortunately, spray everything below two feet high. Yuk! All the nice airflow windows were covered up and the door opening, which only had a curtain, was barricaded and cleaned with vinegar. Exchanging one smell for another, vinegar's not exactly sweet smelling but it's better than tom cat spray.

Apart from the day of the party we had true Galician rain. It hammered every single day, but we stayed dry in our "shed" and it was quite nice in the peace and quiet listening to the rain beat the toughened glass to cleanliness in the ten minutes or so from waking to the mayhem of breakfast for ten.

During one of these ten-minute morning waking-up quiet times, we decided that the shed needed a solid door to keep the cats outside, to provide a bit of security, to keep the driving Galician rain from soaking the floor, and, if we ever have a houseful again, to give us a barrier from our houseguests. At this stage of our renovations, we'd used up most of the timber received from our neighbour and, perish the thought, we might have to buy some. Shock, horror, this was against all we hold dear, and this old "shed" would look awful with a new door, because everything else, except for a new concrete floor, was original, recycled, or old.

The party over, our guests returned to the old lives and we returned the house, garden, and outbuildings to their original function, including the "shed," or project room. Empty, it was a fair-sized room and we were again excited about what we were going to achieve with the projects we will create in this room. It still needed a door and we didn't have any old timbers. However, one of the last tasks was to put away the lovely table top for ten, with its raised centre. "Why not use the timber from this?" I mooted after moving this heavy table top for the 'enth time that day to make space for other stuff. It was duly measured and compared with the opening it was to fill. It could be done.

Using the project room, all fixings, battens, and the raised centre, so lovingly hand sawn, was removed and tidied away for use on another day and project. John's chin was rubbed and scratched, and the pencil stuck under his top lip was chewed whilst he thought. This went on for several days—not continuously mind you. He remained deep in thought. "What else could he incorporate in the door?" "How was he going to fix it?" Rummaging through his treasure trove of metal, wood, and odd found bits, he tormented himself. "Which bits was he going to use?" "Would this work?" "Can I attach this to that?" It was painful to watch. You can bet Simon Starling never had these torments or so much anguish.

Then came the "aha!" moment. In his mind everything had settled into place: the design, the structure, the fixings, including the hows, the whats and the wheres. His next step was to saw, plane, and sand the main pieces of timber without losing any of the blackened, cooking-smoke finish or the live (though they've been dead for many years) edges. Once completed and treated with linseed oil to protect the surface from the blistering sun and the pouring rain, they were clamped together with battens and G-cramps. (Don't ask me what they are, but they did the job.)

The second task, a bit of design work here—he couldn't just have a functioning door now, could he? He marked the iron window grill, which he'd found under piles of rubbish when we were clearing what will be the sheep pen (another story), onto the top third of the timbers and sawed a hole to fit. It did look as if it had been there forever and more like a Wild West jail house than a Galician Alpendre or open barn). The whole piece, clamped, was turned over and the inside or back exposed. The holding together and strength pieces had to be added. These were pieces of chestnut that, in a past life, had held roof slates in place. They were flat along one face, but none were straight or flat along any other. There were three, one at the top, one at the bottom, and a third on the diagonal. And all were drilled and screwed into place. Another coat of Linseed oil was added.

The barrel hoops, which had been hung up in John's workshop for the past four years, were a beautiful rust colour. These were cut at the joining seam and beaten flat. They looked so tactile. The flat metal with slight curve edges, raised rough surface and a rusty colour. These beauties were going to be on the outside or front of the door. They were laid in place onto the clamped timbers, and the holes for the screws were marked.

Holes were drilled and the ornamental metal ex-hoops were screwed into place. To finish the front of the door a sweep was attached. I had to look that up. It's the sticky out bit at the bottom of the door to prevent water coming in and has nothing to do with chimneys. Two large handmade hinges were also attached to the front. This door looked very impressive, but still like the entrance to a jail. The hinges had come off the old timbers from our neighbour.

The door frame, which had been completed a year ago, was cut to form a recess to fit the door into. No cat, draught, or drop of rain will ever enter the project room, ever. I'd like to say the door slotted in beautifully first time, but I'd be telling fibs. There was lots of swearing, huffing, chiselling, scraping, and "Jax give us a hand" before, "Ta-da," it fitted and looked splendid. The pintle (I had to look that name up as well), or the stubby bit that's fixed to the frame to slot the hinge onto, was attached and the door hung. It still looked like a jailhouse. Last, but not least, the lock and handle. The lock, again, was found in a pile of old buried rubbish and didn't have a key. It was very plain, rusty, and large but once disassembled, greased, and reassembled, it worked.

Monforte had a very old ironmongers that probably contained everything you could ever possibly want. Items, priced in pesetas, hung from the ceiling and the columns and lay on a maze of shelving, along with cobwebs. This is where John found blank keys large enough to fit the lock and for the princely sum of one euro. After much sawing, filing, and cleaning with a Dremel this time, the key fitted and the lock turned. Two days work and a euro. The handle was the easiest and prettiest piece rummaged from John's box of old bits of saved and scavenged metal. And finally a last coat of Linseed oil was applied.

The finished door suits the stone project room and looks as if it's been there forever. The hand-forged grill, now painted dark red, allows air to enter but not the local cats. The sweep keeps the driving rain out, the decorative flattened barrel hoops are gorgeous, and the blackened timbers are solid and just right. The hefty key hangs in the kitchen in readiness for the next venture.

~

Our door. Photo by J. P. Vincent.

Día das Letras Galegas

by Jennifer Juan

The sun sets,
Saturday night,
across the sand of Samil beach.
Beauty on the boardwalk,
violet velvet goes from your shoulders,
to mine,
as the night joins us.
We spot ships and stars,
through telescopes,
telling tall tales,
of all the loves that lead to us.
Wish I may,
wish you would,
be mine,
May seventeenth,
my love.
As Vitrasa carries us towards your lair,
I lie in your lap,
knowing I could not write,
a verse half as beautiful as you.

~

A Summer with a Difference

by Andrea Jones Jones

April 2011

"You teach English, don't you?" Susana suddenly asked me. We were standing outside the building where we were attending a training course in administration, having a quick cigarette.

"Yes," I replied guardedly, well aware Susana had three children at primary school. I have been an English teacher since I was eighteen, but I found out very early on that I didn't like teaching children. Happily, the demand has grown so much that I can have a cutoff age of fourteen (although I'm thinking of increasing it to sixteen when some of my current students reach that age).

"Good. I have a cousin who is studying English at the language school in the neighbouring community."

That's a long way to come for classes, I thought to myself, but before I had the chance to comment she continued. "He spends all his summer holiday here in the village. I'll call him and you can talk."

"Just give him my number and he can contact me when he comes for his holidays," I said. I was wasting my breath, as Susana was busy scrolling down to find his number. I thought, What does she expect me to say to him? This isn't how I do things. It's the people who want classes who contact me. I don't go around ringing random strangers touting for business.

Before I could protest, I heard her asking about the family and then saying, "I have a friend here who's an English teacher. Speak to her," as she handed her mobile to me.

"Hello," I said timidly, thinking I really must start standing up to people more. I easily get steamrolled into doing things against my better judgment.

"I am studying English here in my city at the language school, but I'm having difficulty with the oral exam. I don't

107

think I am going to pass my final exam, so I need to prepare to resit for it in September. I spend a month in Galicia so I could come to classes several times a week."

This is familiar territory, so I started to feel confident as I answered, "That's fine. I have numerous pupils who have prepared or are preparing these exams, so I am familiar with the topics. We can have conversation classes and practice speaking about . . ."

"Wait a minute," he interrupted my language spiel. "I want to have classes with a native teacher."

"Yes, I am a native teacher."

"Well, you have a Galician accent."

Did he expect me to apologise? I grew up in Galicia. I'm hardly likely to have an Andalusian accent, am I?

"I can assure you that when I speak English, I don't." I didn't think it wise to mention that when I spoke English I had a very thick black-country accent. This is something I had been blissfully unaware of for thirty years, until I first came into contact with other people from different parts of the UK, and they kindly pointed it out. Many times. Repeatedly.

I was feeling quite cross. Never before had anyone doubted that I was English. I must admit that when Spanish people met me for the first time on translating jobs, they frequently commented how good my English was. I always said, "Thank you. That's nice, but I AM English and that helps a lot." And so far everyone had always accepted my word unreservedly.

Anyway, I didn't have time to dwell on it as we had to go back into classes.

* * * *

July 2012

My phone rang—an unknown number. I hoped it was a prospective student with enquiries as I was trying to fill my gaps for the summer. As I work privately, it's always a bit stressful when I am starting the school year or the summer period until I have enough work to pay the bills and put food on the table. Every year I shiver in trepidation in case I don't get enough classes scheduled and I have to take on some little children.

"Yes?" I asked optimistically.

"Hi. It's Susana's cousin. We spoke last year about English classes for the summer."

Silly me. When we had spoken the previous year, I had mistakenly assumed we were talking about classes for that summer. Now, I always recommend that my students book their classes for the summer in advance, if possible, even if they are going to start later so they can reserve the timetables that suit them best, but fifteen months in advance is a bit extreme.

"Yes, I remember."

"Well, you see," he continued, "last year I passed my exams in the end, so I didn't need them. But this year I failed the oral exam, so I would like to come several days a week to practise."

"That's fine. I have quite a few free hours. So, tell me what timetable suits you and when you would like to start and we can take it from there."

"I'll be there on the 1st of August. And I would like to come for two or three hours a week, in the morning, if possible. You are English, right?"

Oh no, not that again. I felt my hackles rising.

"Yes, I am definitely English. We can start on Monday, the 3rd, at 11:00 am if that suits you. This is my address. Shall I explain how to get here?"

"It's OK. I'll find it. See you on the 3rd."

* * * *

August 2012

The day arrived for our first class. I am always a little nervous when a new student starts. I started to worry about things like: Will we get on? Will the classes be successful? And now I had an extra worry: Will my English pass muster?

I had just sat down when my previous student left, and I thought I had time for a little respite. Spaniards are not normally punctual and most people have difficulty locating my second-floor flat, as the ground floor has a flight of steps to the entrance, which confuses people, and the first time (and sometimes a couple of times more) they invariably ring the first-floor doorbell. Fortunately, my neighbours work all day, so they don't have to redirect many of my students. The cat promptly draped herself round my neck as I sat down in front of the computer. The doorbell rang. I didn't have time to remove the cat. I opened the door to find my new student there.

"Are you Andrea?"

I could feel a slight disapproval, which I wasn't sure was due to the fact that I had a cat draped around my neck or to my Galician accent when I replied, "I am. Come in."

I hastily put the cat on chair under the table and thought what a good job I put the dog in my daughter's room, as he can be a bit effusive and not everyone feels comfortable with big dogs. I came to the conclusion he was not an animal lover as most people coo over how cute my cat is.

"I want to ask you something," he said. Oh, I thought, he is going to ask to see my ID to prove I am English. In the meantime I had found out he was a policeman, which probably explained how he had found my flat so easily.

"I would like to cycle to classes, but I want to know if my bicycle will be safe downstairs as it is a very expensive racing bike."

Lord, give me patience. Now he thinks we're a bunch of crooks in my neighbourhood.

"We have a lock-up downstairs where you could leave your bike while we have our classes. At the moment, I don't have a key because they changed the locks two weeks ago and I haven't yet collected mine. But I will get the key this afternoon and you can borrow it while you are here."

"Would you really do that?" He seemed surprised I provided a solution so easily. "Are you sure you can get the key?"

I sighed inwardly. Are all policemen so disbelieving? I guess it comes with the job.

"I'll tell you what I'll do. I'll get the key, try the lock to make sure it works, check there is space for your bicycle, and ring you this evening to set your mind at rest. Then you can cycle to class tomorrow."

I switched to English and said, "Now tell me about your exams and what kind of topics you have to discuss."

He did a double take. "Wow, I had doubts about you being a real English person, but you are. Your accent is amazing." I've heard black-country accents called many things but never amazing before. From that moment I had his complete attention. I must admit he had mine too. After such a painful start, things went very smoothly. I noticed he had quite nice eyes as his never left mine for the whole hour. And he was quite droll. In fact, he had quite a deep sexy laugh. The first hour was soon over, and I thought, actually, I think this is going to go better than I had imagined.

I sent my daughter to get the key from the president of the community, and we made sure it worked and cleared a space for my student's bicycle. I rang him to say all was set for the following day. I think our efficiency in sorting out the problem impressed him.

The next morning, at 11:00 on the dot, the downstairs doorbell rang.

"It's me," he said.

I was just winding up my previous class, so I said my daughter would come down with the key. Seconds later I heard a really strange noise as if someone with metal tipped high heels was walking up the stairs, and I heard my daughter's voice shyly saying something. They came in and I realised the noise was made by metal cleats on his cycling shoes. I rolled my eyes. This man does nothing by halves. The dog rushed up to greet him and started licking his legs. The dog has an embarrassing fetish for bare feet and legs. Mind you, he did have great legs.

I sensed the disapproval again.

"I see you have a dog, too."

"I'm sorry, he has a thing for bare legs. Silvia will take him into her room."

"Your daughter is sweet." Thank God something met his approval. "She said I could keep the key while I was here. Is that right?"

"Of course. We don't need it. Just give it back the last day of classes."

The class went even better than the previous day, and I found myself inviting him along on Fridays to an informal exchange meeting we hold for Spaniards who want to practise

111

English and for English-speaking people who live here or are on holiday. We have a great time. There are people from many different parts of the UK, and from other countries, such as Australia and the States, and people of all ages and abilities. We barely touched on the topics that were part of the oral exam.

At one point I asked him if he read much in English, and he told me that three years previously one of his colleagues had brought him an English newspaper back from a trip to the UK. He treasured it and reread it from front page to back every summer. It was getting a bit delicate and yellowed from age. However, the first day of his holiday this year he had gone out cycling to come home to find his mother using his precious paper to black-lead the wood-burning stove. She couldn't understand his devastation over an old tatty newspaper. I couldn't help giggling at the picture of it all.

The next day I had to go to Portugal with my family to see my boys off on an adventure. They were migrating to the UK to try and find jobs. It was bittersweet moment. I was so excited for them but sad at how much I was going to miss them, as I knew they wouldn't be able to come back often and I couldn't afford to go over easily to see them. As we were walking back to the car, I saw a small newsagent's shop that sold English newspapers. It reminded me of my student's loss, so I bought him a newspaper. He was delighted.

I started to look forward to our classes more and more, and when I got an unexpected call one afternoon asking me if I was free and if I fancied a coffee, I thought maybe I was not the only one who was enjoying this. I agreed, of course, but said I needed to bring the dog. A brief hesitation and then "Sure, that's fine." I must say the dog was on his best behaviour. He lay peacefully under the table outdoors where we sat and chatted for four hours. It was the first time we had chatted in Spanish, and it was the beginning of a beautiful friendship that lasted for three wonderful summers.

It certainly was a summer with a difference.

~

Working the clay. Photo by https://depositphotos.com/portfolio-1016231.html

Earth Mother

by J. P. Vincent

Wise hands they caressed and smoothed the clay
dipped in water shone, turned the wheel it spun.
Dug from the earth where it will return one day.

She sighed with pleasure began her workday
Sunk thumbs into lump her creation begun.
Wise hands they caressed and smoothed the clay.

Skilfully eased out shapes confined, that lay
curved and ridged with nowhere to run.
Dug from the earth where it will return one day.

Unhurried raised, wheel spun, imagined the day
completed, her creation in kiln and done.
Wise hands they caressed and smoothed the clay.

Time passed, ignored, not heavy it weighed
undertook no labour and never to shun.
Dug from the earth where it will return one day.

A masterpiece? And a smile that lay
under the surface, a union perfected.
Wise hands they caressed and smoothed the clay.
Dug from the earth where it will return one day.

~

A Time to Sow

by Lisa Wright

Galegos are very conservative when it comes to food. This is likely partly a rural thing—not much opportunity to try new flavours and cuisines whilst growing up on a small farm six hours from the nearest curry house—and partly a fiercely Galician pride in their own culture and the food, which is very much a part of it.

A Japanese restaurant opened—very briefly—in our local city. The day we visited there were five of us and four staff. The owner, a lovely chap from Barcelona, was quite cagey when we asked curiously why he had chosen our town. "Because there wasn't a Japanese restaurant here." . . . mmm.

Not that he helped himself. There was no Menu del Dia, no tapas at the bar to try the novel cuisine, which was beautifully presented in the Japanese style but so small! A single prawn on my seven-euro fried rice. Where were the rest of them? And the bread, the vino?

In the allotment it's the same story. We are blessed here in Galicia with a climate suited not only to temperate vegetables, like cabbage and parsnips, but also many Mediterranean ones, like aubergines and peppers. But huerta after huerta grows potatoes, cabbage, corn.

When I picked my mange tout, Iñes asked why I didn't wait until the peas had formed. My cherry tomatoes were considered "a bit small" and my parsnips "animal food".

Slowly things are changing. One year S made me a cloche. The next year Carmen had an identical one. The year I started watering with plastic bottles to get much-needed moisture to the growing plants' roots, the village was suddenly beset by sunlight glinting on upturned plastic bottles in every vegetable patch!

Maybe the locals are willing to learn from *los ingleses*.

Despite their conservancy, most Galegos have very productive gardens and allotments.

In the local market vendors sell bunches of part-grown carrots and onions to plant or bare-rooted cabbage seedlings, which sit wilting in the fierce heat for half the morning before being bought, then left in a scorchingly hot car whilst the purchaser has a leisurely lunch followed by a nice siesta. All the time the delicate fledgling vegetables sit quietly drooping. Then, around 7:00 p.m., the buyer awakens. Down to the newly hoed patch in the huerta he trots. Along each perfect furrow he goes, quickly laying out the cabbagelets, roots toward the valley, limp leaves along the ridge above, then he carefully covers the tender roots and gently waters in the young plants.

Er, no, actually, then he goes indoors for a quick vino and dinner, leaving these young orphan plants exposed and vulnerable to the worst the weather can throw at them. They lie, limp and unloved for three days. Then, deciding they may as well make the best of it, they start to grow, and grow, and grow until they rival Jack's bean stalk in height. In fact, Jack would have been better with a sturdy Galician walking stick cabbage for a climbing frame—though chopping it down could have proved hard work!

For a moment, please, dear reader, I would ask you to consider the tough uncompromising life of a Galego cabbage seedling and compare it with that of my own cabbages.

I sow my seeds, two or three to a pot, in good compost, thinning to one strong seedling and growing this youngster on, still in its own warm cocoon, until it has six good leaves. On a cool day I make a slot in the soil where it is to be planted. Taking care not to disturb it too much, I tap the young plant out, root-ball and beautiful soil clinging to it and protecting the roots. I place it carefully but firmly into its slit, firm the soil, and water it gently. I place a sunscreen to keep it from overheating and cover it if it's a little cool in the evenings. It is, in fact, a mollycoddled, spoilt child of a cabbage. And is it grateful? Does it grow huge, overshadowing my neighbours' latchkey cabbages? Does it return my love and affection by being big and strong and delicious?

Does it heck! My neighbours' cabbages are *rascacielos* and ready for eating while mine are still in nappies being read a bedtime story.

Maybe *los ingleses* still have something to learn from the Galegos too.

~

About the Authors

Adrián Casanova Chiclana

Adrián Casanova Chiclana, Galician born, says he enjoys writing because he considers it a natural and silent means of communication among people who are far apart. Writing is a powerful tool, which can stir up intense feelings and emotions. He usually writes in the Galician language because he believes it is a breath of fresh air, reminiscent of the scent of damp earth after the first drops of rain. He has previously taken part in several competitions in this language, obtaining second place in the Xuventude Crea (2016), a short story competition organized by the Xunta de Galicia and being short-listed in the competition O Lugar Onde Vivo, Relatos polo Territorio (2014), organized by ADEGA Publishing and the Diputation of Lugo. He describes himself as an inquisitive person who has many interests and an entropy lover. For this reason, he belongs to a cultural association called Náufragos do Paradiso, which aims to turn the Ribeira Sacra into a cultural paradise besides being a place of natural beauty, of extensive Romanesque heritage and the cradle of the famous Ribeira Sacra wines. #P.S.:Love the Planet.

Fiona Cowan

Fiona Cowan is from Orkney and has spent most of her life working there as an occuptional therapist. When their two sons set off for university, she and husband, Les Cowan, author of the David Hidalgo crime series, set off as grown-up gappers studying in New Zealand, London, and Madrid. Reaching Galicia in 2013, they taught English, collaborated with a small evangelical church in Ribadeo, and sailed the Rias on sunny days. They have now returned to the Orkneys and she plans to stop blogging, and take more exercise!

Fiona is only motivated to write for competitions and prefers to write in Orcadian, usually poetry. She enjoys the prizes more than seeing her work published or broadcast.

Vanesa de la Puenta Blanco

I was born in Vitoria Gasteiz in 1980, where I still live

I have two children, Izaro and Julen. They are the principal reason I have every day to get up and live, but not the only one: my husband, my parents, my cousin M and the rest of my family and friends are very important for me, too.

My grandparents will be always in my mind and in my heart. I love them.

I love Galicia. I love literature.

I love going through reality to my dreams.

I love loving.

Liza Grantham

Liza Grantham is from England and has lived in Galicia for seven years. She has written for pleasure since childhood, winning her first poetry competition at the age of eleven. As a primary teacher for over twenty years she enjoyed working with children on performance poetry and drama.

Liza loves the tranquillity of life in her remote *aldea*, where she and her husband make a total of only five residents. In addition to the many labours that come with a rustic lifestyle she spends her free time walking her dog, knitting, sewing, compiling cryptic crosswords and writing poetry, drama and memoirs. She has a passion for cooking and creating her own recipes, always on the look-out for new guinea-pigs to join her dinner table!

Dawn Hawkins

Dawn, hails from Doncaster the home of Michael Parkinson. She attended one of the oldest grammar schools in the UK, founded in 1350

She now lives near Sarria, in Galicia northern Spain. Her home is a typical Galician granite farmhouse, bought as a ruin. She and her partner have spent 10 years creating a habitable space and, although not completed, she now has a space to write and follow her other passion, cooking.

She lives with Steve, the love of her life and husband of 40 years. He has the knack of producing coffee at the salient moment. Especially first thing in the morning

They have three sheep who are professional eaters, organic rabbits, ducks and chickens for the table. Tania, Rowan, and Franki, two rescue dogs and a cat, have the run of the garden, orchard, and field and are her early warning system for visitors.

She also writes under the name of A. D. Thorne.

Robin Hillard

Australian Author, Robin Hillard, grew up in Western Australia goldfields and has lived in provincial cities and towns of various sizes during a career spent teaching in Australia, England, and Canada. She has now settled, with her husband, in Toowoomba, which is known as the garden city of Queensland. It is well served with antique shops and provides inspiration for her mystery stories and puzzles. Toowoomba also provides a site for the Australian town of Ridgeway, which features in her mystery novel, *Ridgeway Murder*. Robin also writes science fiction and reviews poetry for *Polestar Magazine*.

Andrea Jones

Andrea Jones was born in the UK but grew up in Galicia. She left the UK at the age of seven with her mother and stepfather and, after traveling throughout Europe and other parts of Spain, they settled in a small village close to the town of Monforte de Lemos. Mother of four, she has lived for different periods in Burgos and other parts of Galicia, including a short time in Muxía on the famous Death Coast. Finally having returned to Monforte de Lemos, she currently works as a teacher of both English and Spanish. She enjoys writing in her spare time.

Jennifer Juan

Jennifer Juan is a cultural melting pot of an artist. She is a writer, a musician, a film maker and a podcast host. A tornado of darkness and delicacy, Juan creates engaging and powerful projects, using a variety of mediums and platforms, each dripping with her signature playful, yet powerful style of writing.

Beginning her journey as an artist as a teenager, Juan graduated from The University of Greenwich in 2013, and began sharing her work on her personal website, *JenniferJuan.com*, posting written poetry and video projects, including the immersive poetry podcast, *Sincerely, Jennifer x*, which has amassed over 15,000 listeners since it began in 2017. She has also released several printed volumes of poetry, including the critically acclaimed *"Home Wrecker"*, and in 2018 *"27, With A White Lighter"*.

Barbara Mitchell

Barbara is 67, and hails originally from the North of England. She spent her working life as a Probation Officer and then a Child Protection Officer. She has lived in Galicia for 16 years with her partner Diana.

Michelle Northwood

Michele travelled the world for twenty years as a professional dancer, magician and fire-eater. When she retired, she went to work in Galicia as a holiday rep. She met her future husband, Randy, in the hotel featured in the story and although the narrative is fictional, the interactions with the tourists did actually take place.

Currently, she lives in a countryside finca in mainland Spain and shares her home with her husband, three dogs, three cats and two terrapins. However, Galicia will always have a special place in her heart and, once a year, she travels back there to visit her in laws.

Michele has a First Class Honours Degree in Modern Languages (English and Spanish) and runs her own Language School where she prepares children and adults for the prestigious Cambridge English examinations.

She has also just published her first book, *'Fishnets In The Far East'* which is an autobiography.

Noelia Roca Jones

Noelia Roca Jones was born to an English mother and Galician father in a small town in the south of the Galician province of Lugo. She grew up listening to the fascinating legends of the darkest Galician folklore. She is a qualified carer and has worked looking after elderly people both privately and in various nursing homes. However, after a placement in a school for children with special needs, she decided to retrain as a nursery teacher. She is currently doing a two-year college course.

She thought this competition was an excellent opportunity to tell other people one of Galicia's most famous legends and hopes to continue writing in the future.

J. P. Vincent

J. P. Vincent is the penname of Jacqueline Suffolk. A bubbly British blonde, Jacqueline now lives in Galicia, with her sainted partner, John. They share life with a Galician cat called Freddie who was found living, with his mum, under their roof. They spend their time renovating their old stone house, rebuilding barns, and also 200 meters of dry stone walling, which to date they've completed about a tenth of. They also have half a mountain to do something with when they run out of other things to do.

Jacqueline loves to travel. She and John spent many years touring Europe in their motorhome, La Gorda, and she loves to write about travelling. Her bus route No.83 article is in the latest edition of the Bradt Travel Guide "Bus Pass Britain." She is also a consultant for Motorhome Monthly Magazine (MMM) where her remit is to answer queries regarding motorhome travel in northern Spain and Portugal.

Lisa Wright

Lisa, together with partner Stewart, moved to Galicia in 2007, giving up a promising career messing about in ponds as an ecologist to grow veggies to eat (when the mice don't get there first); raise..and sometimes sadly lose...chooks and rabbits and renovate houses- two at last count, the second (and definitely final) one for mum Iris who finally agreed to move to galicia in 2014.

The second question friends usually ask ..after, 'where's that?' is 'why did you chose galicia? ' and we have to answer honestly that galicia chose us. We were just walking the camino de santiago and stopped to look at houses, as one does, and that was that. And we are not alone. Others say they were just passing through or travelling elsewhere when they just...stopped. Galicia has that pull.

We married here in 2010 to the delight of our local concello, which gave us a ceramic council plaque to commemorate the occasion, and we feel more at home here than anywhere else we have ever lived.

~

The Good Life in Galicia

Volumes

The Good Life in Galicia (2016)

Buy the e-book here in all formats

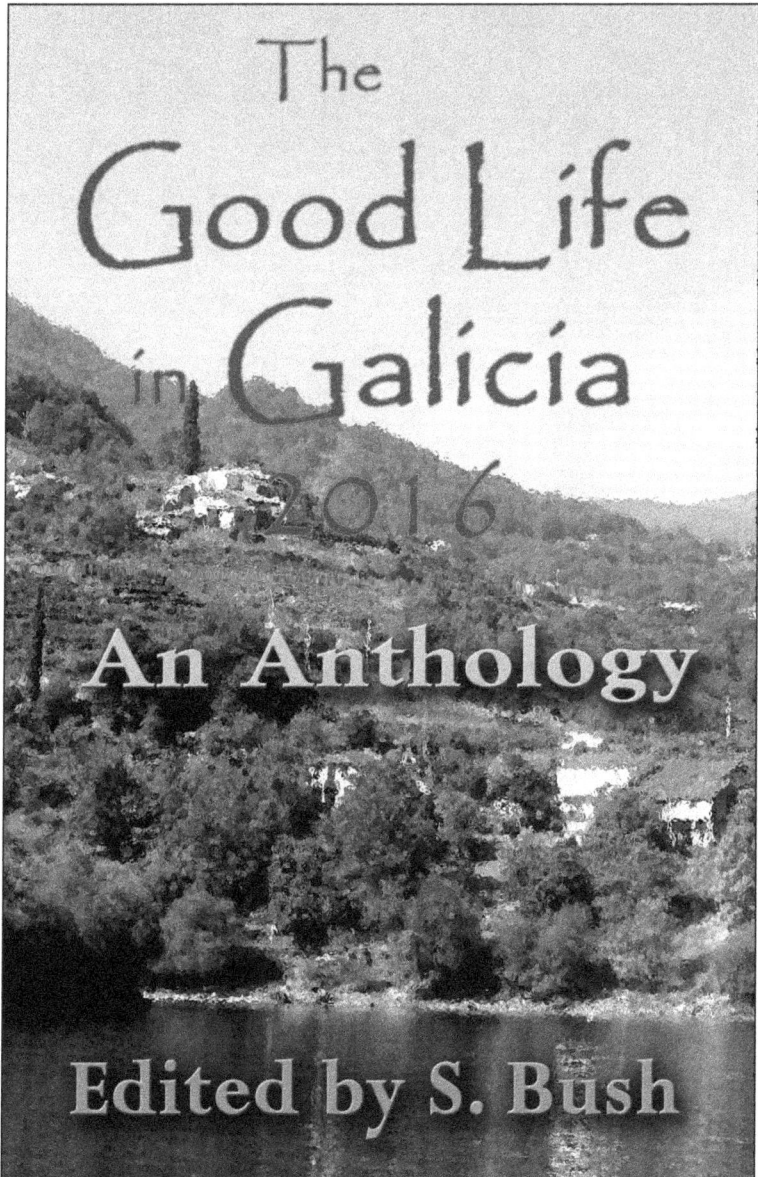

The
Good Life
in Galicia
2016
An Anthology
Edited by S. Bush

The Good Life in Galicia 2017

Buy the e-book here in all formats

https://www.smashwords.com/books/view/783388

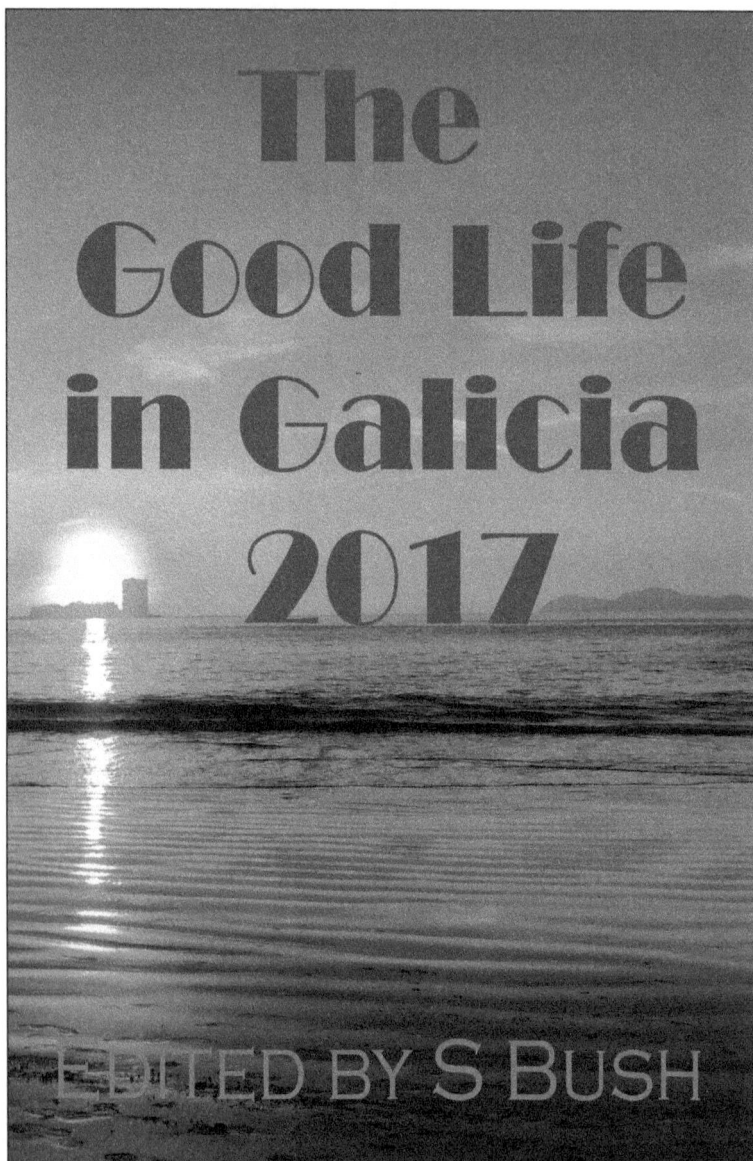

The
Good Life
in Galicia
2017

EDITED BY S BUSH

Cyberworld Publishing

"The Good Life in Galicia" competition 2019
Short story competition and anthology

In 2016 Cyberworld Publishing produced The Good Life in Galicia 2016 after running a competition for short prose pieces in the categories of fiction and nonfiction.

In 2017 we added a poetry category and in 2019 we are again seeking prose pieces in the categories of fiction and nonfiction, and poetry.

Submissions/Entries:

Prose: Fiction and non fiction 1,200 to 4,500 words in
ENGLISH
Poetry: max 20 lines in **ENGLISH**

Prizes: 10 Euros first place and 5 Euros second place in each section, prose fiction, prose non fiction and poetry (paid via Paypal). First place also receives one nights accommodation for two adults at **Casa Campaciñas** vacation houses (conditions apply).

All entries must be available to be published in the anthology "The Good Life in Galicia 2019" in e-book and paperback. Entries to be published will be selected by the volume editors and not all entries may be included (No payments will be made for publication.).

Entries:

- Closing date is 1 August 2019
- All works must be about Galicia in a significant way.

- No requirement for the author/s to have ever been to Galicia
- All entries are to be sent by e-mail to thegoodlifeingalicia2017 ATT outlook dot com
- Entries to be pasted into the e-mail, not sent as attachments.
- All Entries to be in English.
- (Files to in .rtf or .doc 2003 format NO .docx. Font: 12 point Arial. Style: Normal. No Headings style please.)
- Direct all enquiries to thegoodlifeingalicia2017 ATT outlook dot com
- You can find more information and updates for the competition at: www.CyberworldPublishing.com And on Facebook at Cyberworld Publishing

<u>DEADLINE: First of August 2019</u>

~